Game Development Tool Essentials

Alessandro Ardolino, Remi Arnaud, Paula Berinstein,
Simon Franco, Adrien Herubel, John McCutchan,
Nicusor Nedelcu, Benjamin Nitschke, Fabrice Robinet,
Christian Ronchi, Gustavo Samour, Rita Turkowski and
Robert Walter

Game Development Tool Essentials

ISBN-13 (pbk): 978-1-4302-6700-3

ISBN-13 (electronic): 978-1-4302-6701-0

President and Publisher: Paul Manning
Lead Editor: Ben Renow-Clarke
Technical Reviewer: Alan Chaney, Marc Schaerer and Fabrice Robinet
Editorial Board: Steve Anglin, Mark Beckner, Ewan Buckingham, Gary Cornell, Louise Corrigan, Jim DeWolf, Jonathan Gennick, Jonathan Hassell, Robert Hutchinson, Michelle Lowman, James Markham, Matthew Moodie, Jeff Olson, Jeffrey Pepper, Douglas Pundick, Ben Renow-Clarke, Dominic Shakeshaft, Gwenan Spearing, Matt Wade, Steve Weiss
Coordinating Editor: Christine Ricketts
Copy Editor: Mary Behr
Compositor: SPi Global
Indexer: SPi Global
Artist: SPi Global
Cover Designer: Anna Ishchenko

Distributed to the book trade worldwide by Springer Science+Business Media New York, 233 Spring Street, 6th Floor, New York, NY 10013. Phone 1-800-SPRINGER, fax (201) 348-4505, e-mail orders-ny@springer-sbm.com, or visit www.springeronline.com. Apress Media, LLC is a California LLC and the sole member (owner) is Springer Science + Business Media Finance Inc (SSBM Finance Inc). SSBM Finance Inc is a Delaware corporation.

For information on translations, please e-mail rights@apress.com, or visit www.apress.com.

Apress and friends of ED books may be purchased in bulk for academic, corporate, or promotional use. eBook versions and licenses are also available for most titles. For more information, reference our Special Bulk Sales–eBook Licensing web page at www.apress.com/bulk-sales.

Any source code or other supplementary material referenced by the author in this text is available to readers at www.apress.com. For detailed information about how to locate your book's source code, go to www.apress.com/source-code/.

For game developers everywhere

Contents at a Glance

Contents

About the Authors

Paula Berinstein has written numerous how-to books and articles as well as technical documentation for software companies. She produced and hosted The Writing Show podcast from 2005 to 2012. She is currently developing casual games based on elements of her novel *Amanda Lester and the Pink Sugar Conspiracy*.

Nicusor Nedelcu is a game technology researcher and software architect. He's currently CEO of 7thFACTOR Software, which creates game development middleware. He previously worked as editor & tools R&D Software Engineer at Crytek GmbH in Frankfurt am Main, Germany.

Alessandro Ardolino is currently Senior Technical Artist at Ghost Games - EA in Göteborg. He was formerly the Art Technical Director and VFX Artist at Ubisoft Milan studio.

Dr. Rémi Arnaud serves as Principal Member of Technical Staff at AMD, where he leads the effort in web acceleration. His involvement with real-time graphics started in the R&D department of Thales where he designed the Space Magic real-time visual system, and optioned his Ph.D 'La synthèse d'images en temps réel.' He then relocated to California to join Silicon Graphics's IRIS Performer team. He then co-founded Intrinsic Graphics where he designed a middleware for PS2, Xbox, GameCube, and the PC. Later on he served as Graphics Architect of SCEA R&D, working on the PLAYSTATION®3 SDK graphics API. He joined the Khronos Group, contributing to OpenGL ES, and created the COLLADA standard. At Intel he led the Larrabee Game Engine team (a.k.a. Project Offset). More recently he served as Chief Software Architect at ScreamPoint, designing a web technology 5D system to manage entire cities.

Simon Franco is a senior systems programmer at the Creative Assembly. He started programming on the Commodore Amiga by writing a Pong clone in AMOS and has been coding ever since. He joined the games industry in 2000, after completing a degree in computer science. He started at The Creative Assembly in 2004, where he has been to this day. When he's not keeping his daughter entertained, he's playing the latest game or writing games in assembly code for the ZX Spectrum.

Adrien Herubel (@AdrienHerubel) is currently a programmer at Ubisoft Motion Pictures, where he is part of the team working on the Raving Rabbids Invasion TV series. His work is mainly focused on real-time and offline rendering. He teaches OpenGL programming at the Paris-Est University.

John McCutchan is a Software Engineer at Google working on the Dart Virtual Machine. While an undergraduate, John created inotify, the Linux kernel filesystem event notification system used in every Linux distribution and Android phone. After receiving a M.Sc. in Computer Science from McMaster University, John joined Sony Computer Entertainment of America, where he optimized the Bullet Physics library for the PlayStation 3. In 2013, John created a highly-performant SIMD programming model for dynamically compiled languages, such as Dart and JavaScript.

Benjamin Nitschke is the CEO of Delta Engine. He previously worked on www.Soulcraftgame.com (a mobile action RPG), www.ArenaWars.net (an RTS game, the first commercial .NET game), www.RocketCommander.com (a .NET 2.0 open source game), and Xna Racing Game Starter Kit (the most successful and known XNA starter kit). Benjamin has been a Microsoft MVP for XNA/DirectX from 2006 till 2010 and has written XNA books (*Professional Game Development with XNA*, Wiley, 2007). His blog is at http://blog.deltaengine.net.

Fabrice Robinet works for Montage Studio on seamlessly integrating 3D content on the web. He is also the COLLADA Working Group Chair at Khronos and lead for glTF (graphics library Transmission Format). Prior to joining the MontageJS team, Fabrice worked as a Software Engineer at Apple where he co-created the Scene Kit framework.

Christian Ronchi was born in Milan, Italy and graduated from Brera's school of Arts after which he enrolled at the academy of Belle Arti in the Faculty of Painting. In addition, he has obtained a professional certificate for Computer Graphics through the Enaip institute in Milan. The first years of his career were spent as a freelance artist making commercials for various companies, until 2001 when he joined Ubisoft Studios in Milan, where he has been ever since. At Ubisoft, he has been involved in a number of projects, filling a wide array of functions, working with and creating models, animation, lighting, rendering, composition, and visual effects for both real-time and cinematics, just to mention a few.

Gustavo Samour is Senior Software Engineer at Shiver Entertainment in Miami, Florida. He holds a Computer Science degree, and most recently obtained an Advanced Game Development degree after attending The Guildhall at SMU. He is originally from San Salvador, El Salvador.

Rita Turkowski is employed by AMD as a Senior Embedded Gaming Marketing Manager. Rita came to AMD from Unity Technologies where she was the Sales Team Channel Manager for 20 months. While at Unity, Unity had more developer adoption in the game industry than any other game development technology company, ever. She was a Graphics and Media Software Product Manager at Intel from 2007 until December, 2009 working on graphics and game industry software tools. Before that, Rita was the Executive Director of the Web3D Consortium from 2005 – 2007, working on projects internationally for the adoption of ISO 3D standards, as well as establishing joint working group cooperation with related industry consortia such as Khronos, the OGC, and W3C. Earlier in her career, Rita worked with various start-ups in media development, and throughout most the 1990's Rita worked for Apple. She also spent several years working at AT&T Bell Laboratories while attending grad school in the NY metropolitan area at Stevens Institute of Technology. She has undergraduate and graduate degrees in mathematics and computer science, respectively.

Robert Walter is a Software Analyst and Developer at Intentional Software Corporation, Bellevue, WA. Before, he worked as a researcher and lecturer in game and media science for more than four years, where he initiated and headed the International Workshop on Game Development and Model-Driven Software Development in 2011 (Vancouver, BC) and 2012 (Bremen). He co-authored articles about game development for various conferences, including the International Conference on the Foundations of Digital Games (2010, Monterey, CA) and the International Conference on Advances in Computer Entertainment Technology (2011, Lisboa). With the open-source project DialogScriptDSL, he provides a free-to-use tool to model interactive dialog for video games using textual modeling languages.

About the Technical Reviewers

Marc Schärer is an interactive media software engineer delivering interactive learning, training, and entertainment experiences to mobile, desktop, and web platforms for customers from all over the through his company Gayasoft (www.gayasoft.net), located in Switzerland.

He uses Unity, which he has been using since the 1.x days in 2007, and he enhances its capabilities through extensions where suitable. Marc has a strong background in the 3D graphics, network technology, software engineering, and interactive media, which he started working in as a teenager and later solidified by taking Computer Science and Computational Science and Engineering classes at Swiss Federal Institute of Technology Zürich. This knowledge found usage at Popper (www.popper.org), an interactive 3D behavioral research platform by a Harward powered by Unity, Mathlab, and the ExitGames Photon platforms developed by Gayasoft. With the advent of serious games, Marc is currently focusing his and his company's efforts to research options and technologies for the next generation of interactive and immersive experiences through AR and VR technologies (Metaio, OpenCV, Oculus Rift) and new forms of input (Razer Hydra, Leap Motion).

Alan Chaney started down the technology path years before he knew anything about software. A guy who's always been fascinated by how things work, he fed his curiosity by disassembling everything from clocks to motorcycles. When he learned that software offered the same sort of intellectual stimulation, but without the solder burns, he quickly changed his focus from rewiring objects to writing code. During his career as an engineer and entrepreneur Alan has dedicated himself to reinventing everything from search algorithms to 3D content management, always focused on doing things better, faster, and more elegantly than previously imagined.

Acknowledgments

The authors and editor would like to thank everyone at Apress who helped produce this book. Thanks especially to Lead Editor Ben Renow-Clarke for his support of our idea, and Coordinating Editor Christine Ricketts for holding our hands during the technical review and production processes. Our gratitude also to technical reviewers Remi Arnaud, Alan Chaney, Fabrice Robinet and Marc Schaerer; copy editor Mary Behr; cover designer Anna Ishchenko; and compositor/indexer/artist SPi Global.

Editor Paula Berinstein would like to thank all the chapter authors for their hard work, dedication, and good humor throughout a long, sometimes arduous journey. You guys are the best!

Introduction

The computer game industry isn't what it used to be. Early on, which wasn't all that long ago, developers focused on bringing the magic of arcade games to microcomputers, which was fun, but suffered from a computing environment that was technically and artistically limiting. However, as computing power exploded, so did developers' technical options and creativity, culminating in the sophisticated AAA titles that became so popular in the aughts. These marvels required large development teams, with complex and proprietary platforms that themselves required dedicated teams of programmers, and game development grew up; boy, did it.

In the last few years there has been a massive explosion in the growth of mobile and casual gaming, which has dramatically changed the nature of game development. Many successful products are now developed by small teams that do not have the resources to build the kind of complex tool chains AAA teams use. These developers cannot afford the luxury of specializing in one small part of a complex system. To build a modern game, typically in a web or mobile environment, you must be familiar with a wide range of technologies and techniques, and you must be able to turn your hand to meet the immediate need, which may be just about anything: one day asset management, the next capturing usage statistics, the day after passing conformance tests.

This book was written with the needs of the new developer in mind. We offer strategies for solving a variety of technical problems, both well-known and unusual ones, that our experts have encountered. There's quite a lot about COLLADA, as well as techniques for using the Web and the cloud in your pipeline, rapid prototyping, managing your files and assets, and optimizing your GUIs. We think there's something for everyone here and hope you agree.

Code samples are written in Java, MAXScript, Objective-C, Python, HTML, JavaScript, JSON, C, C++, C#, AngelScript, Xtext, and domain-specific languages.

We've divided the book into four parts:

- Asset and Data Management

- Geometry and Models

- Web Tools

- Programming

Asset and Data Management covers the critical issue of managing your assets in the game development pipeline. Two different aspects are described; both will help developers reduce their workload in the always daunting process of not only organizing original assets, but also tracking changes and versions. For example, Chris Ronchi's "Where Is It" chapter explains why it's important to follow a consistent and thought-through naming strategy and demonstrates how to create one. This basic but useful chapter attacks an area that involves no programming and no expenditure, but can help you save time and money just by using a basic "convention over configuration" approach.

The second section, Geometry and Models, focuses heavily on the COLLADA document format, describing how it can be used to bridge the gap between proprietary high-end tools and the requirements of small developers.

The Web Tools section offers hints on moving game development tools to the cloud as well as some particularly interesting ways in which readily available open source web development tools may be used. By adopting software like Django, for example, it's possible to build a comprehensive web-based gameplay monitoring and tracking system.

Finally, the Programming section offers help for developers who want to create their own flexible workflows. The emphasis here is on employing programming techniques that were originally developed to solve more general problems, such as the Command Pattern and the use of domain-specific languages (DSLs), to simplify the programming task. Each programming chapter describes not only the use, but the concepts behind the particular technique, so you can identify a variety of use cases and build up your armory of skills.

Just a quick word about the development of this book. Unlike almost every game development volume out there, this one was originally published independently by a group of experimenters—people with something to say who came together to try something new; it was titled *Game Tool Gems*. We self-published the book in both hard copy and ebook formats and sold it through Amazon. But it was a bit bare bones: no index, tech reviewed only by each other, laid out by editor Paula B. rather than by a fancy designer. But people liked it, including Apress's editors, and that's how this book with its new title, *Game Development Tool Essentials*, was born. Apress took the basic material, tech reviewed it six ways from Sunday, added that missing index, and expanded and updated all the chapters. And for that, we are most grateful.

We feel that it's critical to share information about the tools we use to create games. The better our knowledge, the faster and more efficiently we can work, and the more cool things we can do. That's why we wrote this book pooling the knowledge and experience of working developers. That fragile pipeline has plagued us long enough. Let's show it who's boss.

## PART 1

Asset and Data Management

CHAPTER 1

■ ■ ■

Plug-in–based Asset Compiler Architecture

Nicuşor Nedelcu

From the beginning of the game creation process to the end, developers have two things to worry about: code and data (game art and other type of assets). In the past, data was formatted specifically for the one platform the game was about to run on. Now we have to format the same data for many different platforms. In order to satisfy this new requirement, we need access to source assets that can be compiled into a variety of targets. We also have more work to do, since special care has to be taken for each format.

However, there are ways to reduce the pain involved in this more complex pipeline. To make this process as streamlined as possible, I propose a plug-in–based asset compiler that can load converter plug-ins for the given asset types. The plug-in–based nature of the compiler can also help developers create their own plug-ins for any other special asset types they need. In this chapter, I describe how to set up and code such a compiler using an example of a texture converter/compiler plug-in. The platform you are going to use is Windows and the language is C++; with few modifications regarding the OS specifics, the code should work on other environments and can even be adapted to other languages.

Design

The underlying plug-in loading system can be a "traditional" dynamic-link library (DLL[1]) loading and querying for the proper interfaces. You will be using the Windows DLL API, but the code is almost the same for other operating systems. The DLL can export a special function that will return an instance of the converter interface (see Listing 1-1). The same goes for other platforms (OS/X, Linux), using their specific dynamic link library API implementations.

Listing 1-1. Creating the Asset Converter Instance Using the Exported DLL Function

```
DLL_EXPORT AssetConverter* createAssetConverter();
```

The interface of the asset converter looks like Listing 1-2.

---

[1]Wikipedia. "Dynamic Link Library." http://en.wikipedia.org/wiki/Dynamic-link_library.

Listing 1-2. The Asset Converter Interface

```
class AssetConverter
{
public:
  enum EType
  {
    eType_Unknown = 0,
    eType_Compiler = 0>>1,
    eType_Importer = 1>>1,
    eType_ImporterCompiler
                    = (eType_Compiler | eType_Importer)
  };

  AssetConverter(){}
  virtual ~AssetConverter(){};
  virtual bool convert(const char* pSrcFilename, const char* pDestPath, const Args& rArgs) = 0; //
Args class is a command line argument parser, not shown here. Basically holds a list of arguments
and their values
  virtual const char* supportedExtensions() const = 0;
  virtual EType type() const = 0;
};
```

The asset converter has a type that represents what the converter does with the given input file: compiles or converts. You make this distinction between compilers and converters because you would like to use compilers to compile data from your intermediate format to the final platform-optimized format, and converters to convert from third party formats to your intermediate format. An example of a compiler is cube.json (the intermediate format) to cube.mesh (final optimized format); of a converter, cube.fbx to cube.json.

You can also have a compiler and a converter in one implementation (flag eType_ImporterCompiler) that can handle third party and intermediate formats (for example, a TextureConverter that converts third party JPG/PNGs and compiles to a custom format like .TEX).

The convert method is the one called by the asset compiler executable when the given command-line arguments are passed to it, and they match the file extensions returned by the supportedExtensions() method. This function should return something like a file mask such as *.jpg, *.tga, *.png, or *.texture, so even a simple substring matching test can select the right converter(s). The command line arguments are shared for all the converters; each one can pick up its own arguments and their values.

By convention, the converters will be called first on the given assets, and after that you will call the compilers. Since you (probably) generated/converted assets from the previous step, now you can compile those intermediate formats into final binary optimized ones for specific platforms.

The main asset compiler executable will load all plug-in DLLs from either a specific folder or the same folder as the executable. You can use any kind of plug-in loading scheme. For example, you can have those DLLs with their extensions named .plugin, .converter, etc. In this way, you dynamically load only the eligible ones, skipping the unsupported/unknown DLLs.

Once a plug-in is loaded, you retrieve the address of the DLL exported createAssetConverter() function and instantiate the converter. Then, with all plug-ins loaded, you match each input asset filename with the return string of the supportedExtensions() of each converter. If the match is true, then you call the converter to take care of that file type. After that, you can continue to pass the filename to be handled by other matching converters, or you could come up with a stop Boolean return value so the file will be handled only once by a single converter and not by further matching converters if the return value is false. Even further, you could have some sort of dependency tree dictating when converters would be called after others have finished converting assets.

Obviously, another thing that speeds up the compilation/conversion process is multithreading.[2] In a first phase, you can schedule groups of files to be converted on separate threads. Then, when you convert a few files, the converters could spawn several threads to take care of a single asset. You must be sure, however, that the available cores are used/spread evenly, whether on a CPU or GPU.

Multithreading asset compilation can be a little tricky when dependencies are involved, so for this process to be safe, and to avoid problems arising from two threads concurrently modifying the same resource, you should build a dependency tree and put each main branch and its sub-branches and/or leaves on their own thread. Various methods for thread synchronization can be used, like mutexes and semaphores, each operating system having its own API for that. The main compiler class would look like Listing 1-3.

Listing 1-3. The Asset Compiler Class

```
class AssetCompiler
{
public:
  AssetCompiler();
  virtual ~AssetCompiler();

  bool compile(const Args& rArgs);
  void compileFolder(
    AssetConverter::EType aConverterType,
    const char* pMask,
    const char* pExcludeMask,
    const char* pCompileFolder,
    const char* pDestFolder);
protected:
  vector<AssetCompilerWorker> m_workerThreads;
      . . . . . . . . . . . . . . . . . . . . .
};
```

The main asset compiler class has the compile(...) method (synchronous call; it will wait until every asset compile thread finishes), which will take the actual command-line arguments. The compileFolder(...) method (asynchronous call; it will just start the threads) will process a given folder for a specific converter type, with a filename mask, an excluding mask, the actual compile folder, and destination folder for the output files. The class also has some worker threads for multithreaded processing of the input assets.

Example

The code in Listing 1-4 shows an example—a texture converter/compiler plug-in.

Listing 1-4. The Texture Converter and Compiler

```
class TextureConverter : public AssetConverter
{
public:
  TextureConverter();
  ~TextureConverter();
```

---

[2]"Multithreading." http://en.wikipedia.org/wiki/Multithreading_(computer_architecture).

```
  bool convert(const char* pSrcFilename, const char* pDestPath, const Args& rArgs);
  const char* supportedExtensions() const
{
    return "*.jpg *.png *.psd *.tex";
}
  EType type() const
{
   return eType_ImporterCompiler;
}
};
```

As you can see, the texture converter plug-in class will return all supported file extensions and their types, so the main compiler class will select it when appropriate.

Inside the convert method, the code will check the input filename and dispatch the logic to the specific image format handler.

This class can reside in a DLL, and you can have a single converter per DLL, but you can also have as many converter classes in a DLL as you want. In that case, the query function will just have to change to support multiple classes. See Listing 1-5.

Listing 1-5. A Plug-in with Multiple Converter Classes Inside a Single DLL

```
// this class must be implemented by the plug-ins
class AssetCompilerPlugin
{
virtual int getClassCount() = 0;
virtual AssetConverter* newClassInstance(int aIndex) = 0;
}
DLL_EXPORT AssetCompilerPlugin* createPluginInstance();
```

The exported createPluginInstance() will create the plug-in's class instance, which will take care of instantiating converter classes.

Other converter plug-in examples include an FBX converter, mesh compiler, prefab compiler, shader compiler, MP3/OGG/WAV converter, level compiler, etc. The plug-in system can be developed further with class descriptors, so you can have information about the converter classes without having to instantiate them unless they are needed.

Conclusion

Making the asset compiler modularized can yield huge benefits: shorter development time, the ability to extend and debug the tool, and happy third party developers who will use the tools since they can implement new converters/compilers for their custom data file formats.

Keep in mind optimizations like multithreading; dependency trees; CUDA/GPGPU operations to speed things; a CRC-based last-modified file info database so you can skip assets that haven't changed; and even safely running many compiler executables on the same data folders.

The solution can be implemented in various ways. The converter ecosystem can be detailed as needed so it will fit perfectly into the game engine's pipeline.

CHAPTER 2

■ ■ ■

GFX Asset Data Management

Christian Ronchi

Working in a software house is primarily about collaborating with other people, so the first thing to do when you start a new project is set up a pipeline that facilitates the flow of assets and information. Ignoring this important preparation can create confusion and waste time during production, so you want to make sure you do it right.

One of the most important considerations in setting up such a pipeline is keeping track of your assets. You don't want programmers and artists making changes to the wrong version, or losing the best version, or not being able to find that great character variation to show the director who needs to see it right now. Fortunately, it's not difficult to create a system that will keep these kinds of disasters from happening. What you need is

- One place for everything. Assets and project information should be stored centrally to keep them consistent. You might want to use a wiki or set up a common space (sometimes we use Microsoft SharePoint in our studio) where information can be constantly updated and available.

- Easy-to-understand file names and organization. Asset naming conventions, folder structures, and file organization must be simple, efficient, and intuitive.

This chapter focuses on the second element of that system: file organization and naming conventions.

Folder Structure

Folder structures, file names, and their internal organization must be designed to be clearly interpretable by any person who needs to work with the project's assets. Figure 2-1 shows an example of bad organization of the directory structure/files applied to a common type of Autodesk 3ds Max project. Next to it, in Figure 2-2, you can see the same project with a simple, well-organized structure. In this example, we're using a train station with a palm tree.

7

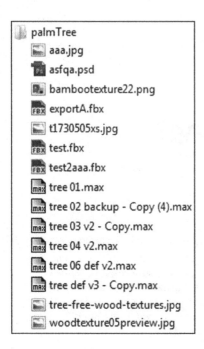

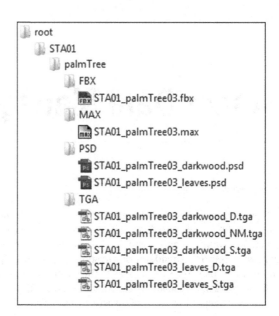

Figure 2-1. *(left). A badly organized structure*   ***Figure 2-2.*** *(right). A clearly organized structure*

At first glance, the structure on the left (Figure 2-1) might seem the best solution, since it is definitely faster (everything resides in a single directory), but in practice, it is surely the most discouraging and inconvenient setup for a person who has no previous experience with the project. Grouping all the palm tree files into one folder and listing them alphabetically doesn't impose any logical structure on the information. Because files used for different purposes are thrown together, the user must go through a process of trial and error, scanning every name and guessing at each file's purpose. Imagine doing that all day.

The structure on the right (Figure 2-2) makes it easy to understand where to find all the files needed for the project, and their purpose. Files are grouped together by how they will be used and arranged hierarchically. Just like your object-oriented code, this kind of file structure is logical and depends on the relationships among assets. It takes a bit of extra thought to set up your structure this way, but the investment is worth it in time saved and frustration avoided. Even someone unfamiliar with the project could pinpoint a specific file in no time with this kind of organization.

Figure 2-3 shows the basic structure I usually use. The elements are

- Root: The root of your project

- Map name: The name of the layer where you'll put the models and textures for your objects

- Obj name: The name of the 3D object

- FBX: 3D model export in FBX format

- MAX: Source file of the 3D model

- PSD: Source files used for this model

- TGA: Exported texture files in TGA format used for the 3D model

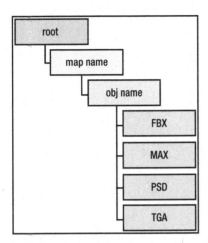

Figure 2-3. *A basic folder structure for a common 3D project*

You can expand on this scheme, of course. For example, if you have video files, Adobe After Effects projects, and sequences rendered from 3ds Max, you can add folders, as shown in Figure 2-4.

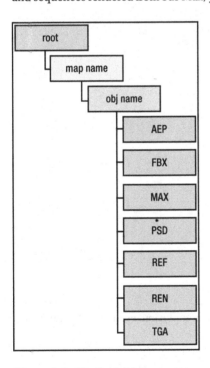

Figure 2-4. *The basic folder structure expanded to a more "render-oriented" setup*

Sometimes you will have items such as textures or render sequences of images that are shared by multiple projects. In this case, you should use a common folder (see Figure 2-5) to store your shared content. Or, opt for the most expensive choice (in terms of space) but more convenient because it creates fewer dependencies: duplicate your content in the folders of the projects where they are used. For example, if the object STA01_palmTree03 shares one or more textures with the object STA01_oakTree01, the textures would be found in the folders of both objects.

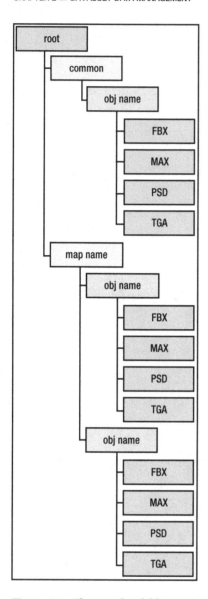

Figure 2-5. *The complete folder structure of the project, also with the common tree*

Avoid using linked references to other projects, as this practice usually creates confusion, even though it might save on disk space (which really isn't a big problem anymore).

Naming Conventions

When naming files, I usually use a system that includes the name of the asset and a prefix indicating the name of the map to which it belongs. You can choose the number of characters to use; my advice is do not overdo it and be as brief as possible without having too many restrictions. Since most projects contain a vast amount of assets, in order to avoid a "wall of text" effect, it's very important to maintain a very short, easy-to-read naming convention. A prefix with a length of 3-5 characters is ideal.

3D Models

When you are working with 3D models, always save both source files and exports; never keep only the export because it may contain only a reduced version of your model. For example, some scripts, rigs, or animation content might not be saved in the export file.

However, in either case, the naming conventions are the same. Suppose that you're working on a map that has a setting for a train station. The suffix might look something like this:

`STA01_palmTree03`

This sample suffix is organized as

- <map name>_<object name><incremental number>, where
    - <map name> is the name of the map that shows the location of the object (`STA01`).
    - <object name> is the name chosen for the object (`palmTree`).
    - <incremental number> is the number of the object version (for example day/night state or split into two chapters) (`03`).

You may also need to add a category for the object. My suggestion is to keep it short (three characters are enough in most cases), as in

`STA01_VEG_palmTree03`

As you can see, most of the suffix is the same as before, but I have inserted the category after the map name. This suffix breaks down as follows:

- <map name>_<category>_<object name><incremental number>, where
    - <map name> is the name of the map where the object is (`STA01`).
    - <category> is the category of the object, in this case the abbreviation of vegetation (`VEG`).
    - <object name> is the name chosen for the object (`palmTree`).
    - <incremental number> is the number of the object variation (`03`).

In addition to constructing solid file naming conventions, you should create a clean and well-organized internal structure of your `.max` file.

In Figure 2-6, in addition to the 3D model, there is a mini-rig to procedurally control certain properties, like the three measurements of the table (height, width, and depth) and the color of the glass material. Layers are used to define which visual objects are part of the mesh, and which are control objects to help the mini-rig.

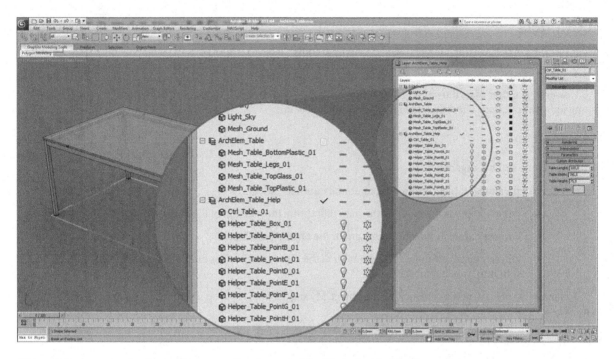

Figure 2-6. *An example of a naming convention for a model with rig, inside 3ds Max*

The naming convention here is slightly different from what I've described above, but the goal is the same: to immediately understand the purpose of the objects in the scene.

Textures

For textures as with 3D models, you must always maintain the source files together with the exports. Image file names and folders need to be as clear, simple, and well organized as those for 3D models.

Texture naming conventions are based on the characteristics of the textures. Names include the kind of object, the type of material, and a suffix that indicates the channel type in which they will be applied.

I use the following abbreviations (see Figure 2-7):

- _D: diffuse map

- _S: specular map

- _NM: normal map

- _HM: height map or displacement map

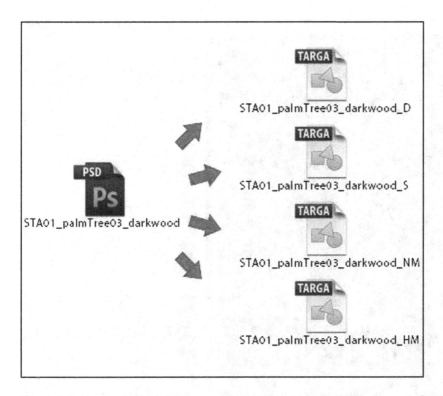

Figure 2-7. *From a single .psd file, you will create the textures for all the channels (diffuse, specular, normal map, and height map)*

In Figure 2-8, you can see that some folders are used to divide the layers according to their channel usage when exported, in order to group the parts that require a combination of multiple layers and layer colors in order to help the division within the folders.

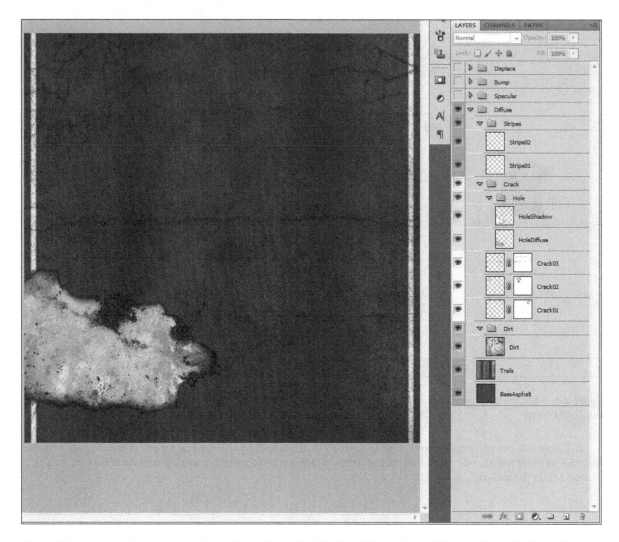

Figure 2-8. *An example of organization within a Photoshop file. The folder and the different colors help the reading of the file*

You might also want to categorize by Smart Object, which introduces the concept of instances inside Adobe Photoshop. Modifying one Smart Object updates all the linked instances, which means that you can use that feature to easily change all the buttons of your ingame menu, or apply nondestructive transformations to some layers without losing your original image data. For more information about the Smart Object feature, see http://help.adobe.com/en_US/photoshop/cs/using/WSB3154840-1191-47b7-BA5B-2BD8371C31D8a.html#WSCCBCA4AB-7821-4986-BC03-4D1045EF2A57a.

Trying to maintain multiple versions of the file you're working on, or incremental variations of the file name, is often a cause of chaos. At best you can lose time searching for a particular version; at worst you can make intricate changes to the wrong file, hold everyone up, and miss deadlines.

To solve this problem, you need a versioning system, such as Perforce, which will give you a revision history. With such a system in place, you can always roll back to a previous version, and you will solve three problems:

1. You always have the latest version of the file available.

2. You can return to any version you want at any time.

3. You will have a consistent backup of your data.

Of course, an infrastructure with Perforce is not for everyone. A good alternative I use every day is a cloud system like Dropbox or SugarSync, which provides enough functionality for most situations. GitHub is another popular version control system.

Conclusion

In this chapter, I wanted to show the organization system that I most frequently use for my projects. However, this is not the only way; it's just one possibility. The most important thing is clarity; without it, the quality of the work will undoubtedly suffer.

Some small rules that should be never forgotten:

*   Always write in English, so anyone can understand.

*   Spend the required amount of time to organize your work and your data.

*   Making your work easy and clear will help not only you, but also anyone who takes over the project.

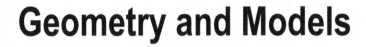

## PART 2

Geometry and Models

■ ■ ■

## CHAPTER 3

Geometry and Models: 3D Format Conversion (FBX, COLLADA)

Benjamin Nitschke
Kirsten Grobe-Nitschke

In this chapter we will discuss several popular 3D model formats used in games and show how to convert and import them.

Although a range of usable formats exists, most tools, engines, and libraries support the now de facto standard FBX and COLLADA (.dae) file formats as well as various ways of importing static geometry (e.g., via OBJ files). While COLLADA had the edge a few years ago, FBX is now pretty much the default 3D model import format in most engines and content creation tools (Unity, Unreal, Maya, 3ds Max, etc.). Both COLLADA and FBX are very powerful and extensible, which means they will remain the most popular 3D export formats for many more years to come.

After we discuss exporting with the most popular 3D content creation tools (3ds Max, Maya, and Blender) and go through the different 3D model formats, we will show the typical workflow for getting 3D meshes and animations into a sample game called Labyrinth. In order to deploy the game to Windows, iOS, Android, and Windows Phone 7, we will be utilizing our DeltaEngine.net technology. The Delta Engine (`http://DeltaEngine.net`) is an open source game engine, written in .NET, but also available in C++ and other languages in the future. It simplifies the process of importing content (2D, 3D, multimedia, etc.). It allows you to deploy games or applications to a bunch of different platforms without having to know a lot of detail about them.

The Sample Game

In the sample game, Labyrinth, you run around a maze with a little dragon trying to find the exit without getting destroyed by a spiky ball rolling towards you. The game runs on Windows, iPhone, iPad, Android phones, Android tablets, and the Windows Phone 7. It features four different 3D models:

- The Dragon character

- The enemy Spikeball that is trying to kill the Dragon

- The maze, which is surrounded by Walls and has pathways

- And finally, Boxes that must be destroyed to advance.

Exporting from 3ds Max

Let's start with the most popular 3D tool for games: Autodesk 3ds Max. At the time of this writing, 3ds Max 2014 had just been released, but you will find that exporting has not changed much in the last five years. Most 3D models we have exported and used in the last years utilized the FBX 2011 format, which works fine with the latest FBX SDK (2014.1). If you use an older version of 3ds Max, the FBX exporter might be a little outdated; check to see if an update is available. Otherwise, try exporting with a COLLADA plug-in[1] instead, or just use the OBJ or 3ds formats for static geometry.

As an example, we'll show how to export the Spikeball 3D model using the FBX format. After the artist has built the geometry and is ready to give his creation to the programmers, your team will have to find a good workflow to let the artist test and play around with different settings, materials, and shader settings without distracting the programmers too much. We recommend setting up as much as possible in the 3D tool. In this case, the artist wants to know how the Spikeball will look in the game. A good way to approximate that situation is to use the exact same shader and rendering technique in 3ds Max, scaling the viewport to the target device resolution, and moving and scaling the model around the way it should look in the game. To render in the same way as with the Delta Engine, the shader file from the Delta Engine Learn web site DeltaEngineSimpleShaderForMax2010-2014.fx is used.[2]

Figure 3-1 shows how to assign a DirectX shader in 3ds Max X via the material editor. Make sure to load the shader .fx file and set up the parameters as shown in Figure 3-1. In our sample game, all we need is the diffuse texture plus a directional light source. Please note that working without a DirectX shader does no harm in this simple case. The 3D model will look pretty much the same with the default material and rendering of 3ds Max, but using your own shader will still help you resolve shader and material issues early and will train your artist to know what is possible and what has not been implemented yet.

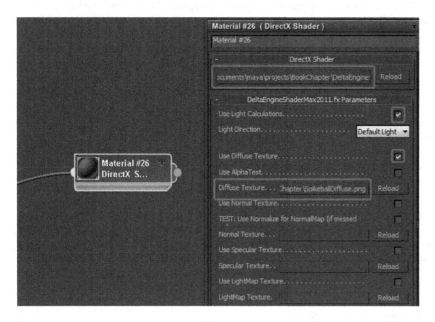

Figure 3-1. *Setting up a DirectX shader in 3ds Max*

---

[1]NetAllied Systems GmbH. http://opencollada.org.
[2]Delta Engine Content Import and Creation. http://deltaengine.net/learn/content-import-creation.

With the material assigned, the selected object can be exported now as an Autodesk (*.fbx) file using the File ➤ Export ➤ Export Selected menu entry (see Figure 3-2). In the FBX Export dialog, certain settings are important.

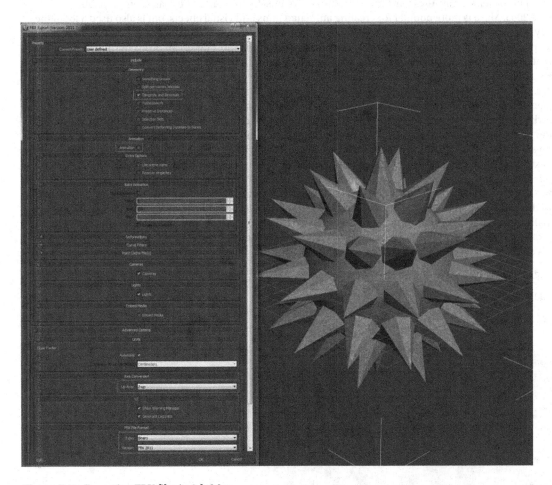

Figure 3-2. *Exporting FBX files in 3ds Max*

If you use normal or parallax mapping, make sure to export Tangents and Binormals. Those can still be generated by the importer, but exporting them here will avoid generating wrong tangents and allow fine-tuning.

If you also want to save animation data, make sure to check the Animation box. In our case, only the Dragon model uses animation.

When animation data is used, select Bake Animation to make sure your importer does not have to calculate all animation matrices, which could slow down importing and rendering. If you like to use key frames and bake matrices yourself, turn the bake option off. Also make sure your start and end time frame is set up correctly.

The Delta Engine uses Z up as the up axis. Make sure to use the same setting here (it's the default for 3ds Max anyway).

Finally, select the latest FBX version (2014.1) and use the Binary format. The text format is also useful if you need to diagnose FBX import issues.

Exporting from Maya

Maya was originally developed by Alias|Wavefront (now Alias Systems Corporation), but has been owned by Autodesk since 2005. Maya is more popular for creating animated films and visual effects, but is also used a lot in the game industry. While these tools originally emphasized slightly different features and functionalities, now they are becoming more and more similar. Even though the interfaces are different, most tasks can be accomplished in pretty much the same way. For example, assigning shader parameters or exporting FBX models in Maya is pretty much the same process as described in the previous section.

There are important differences between the tools, however, and using both tools on the same team can lead to serious headaches, which is why most game teams choose one and stick with it. Exporting and importing static geometry works fine in most tools and is something artists do a lot in everyday work. For example, they might sculpt in ZBrush and rig the result in Maya, 3ds Max, Blender, or LightWave. Going back and forth works fine as long as static geometry (no animation, no material, no shaders, etc.) is used. OBJ, which contains static geometry and nothing else, is a popular exchange format that can be used for this purpose.

The main reason for the incompatibilities of the different 3D tools is the way geometry and scenes are set up. While 3ds Max uses Z as the up axis, Maya prefers Y as the up axis, and most scenes in a game created with the latter will be set up this way. You can change the up axis after the fact, but all your geometry will be rotated and look wrong, so this is usually not a good idea. Also, if you want to use Maya for DirectX shaders, be careful, as it is not set up for this out of the box. Go to Window ➤ Settings/Preferences ➤ Plug-in Manager and enable the following plug-ins to enable HLSL shaders and .dds textures support in Maya (see Figure 3-3):

- `cgfxShader.mll`

- `ddsFloatReader.mll`

- `HLSLShader.mll`

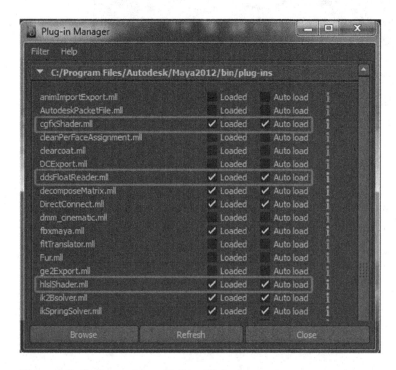

Figure 3-3. *Setting up Maya for DirectX shaders*

Now you can create an HLSL shader material with the hypershade editor (Window ➤ Rendering Editors ➤ Hypershade). Assign this material either by clicking the middle mouse button and dragging the shader node onto the model, or use the right mouse button and choose Assign Material to Selection from the menu (see Figure 3-4).

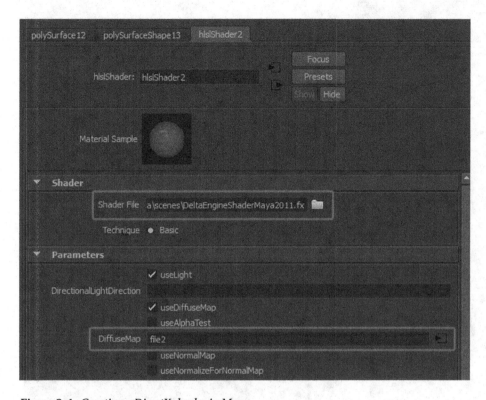

Figure 3-4. *Creating a DirectX shader in Maya*

Maya and 3ds Max shader rendering behave a little different from each other, so a different file has to be used: `DeltaEngineShaderMaya2011.fx`. Everything else works pretty much the same way as with 3ds Max. You can set up the shader parameters as before.

Exporting FBX files is also pretty much the same experience as with 3ds Max (see Figure 3-5). Even when setting the Z up axis in the FBX export dialog, the resulting FBX file will respect the original up axis at the time the scene was created (most likely Y up in Maya), which is something the FBX importer of your game or engine has to be aware of.

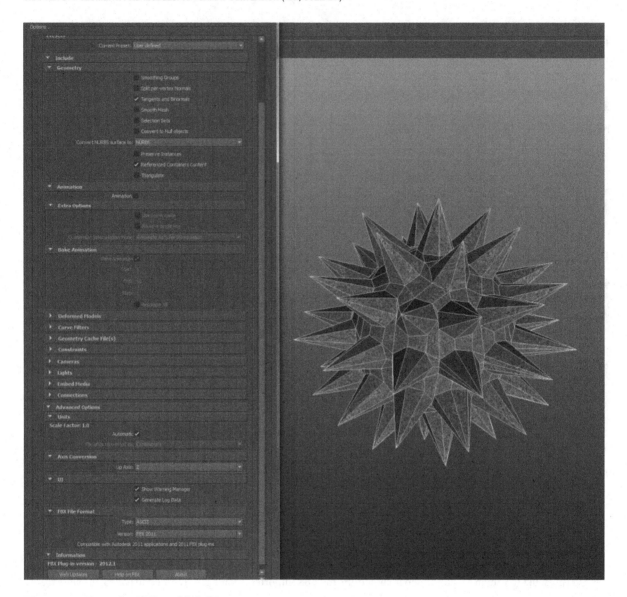

Figure 3-5. *Exporting FBX models in Maya*

Exporting from Blender

Blender is a great alternative to 3ds Max and Maya because it is open source and free to use, as opposed to the expensive packages from Autodesk, which can be a bit much for indie developers. Blender also supports exporting to the FBX file format, and materials can be set up to consume GLSL shaders, but we are not experienced with Blender, and using DirectX shaders does not work out of the box. Still, if you want to set up your render pipeline in Blender, it is possible to create GLSL shaders to make sure the artist sees the same rendering output in Blender as the game uses. If you want the Delta Engine shaders converted to Blender, contact us in the Forum: http://Forum.DeltaEngine.net.

You can, of course, still create 3D models in Blender and export them via the built in FBX exporter functionality (see Figure 3-6). As far as importing goes, please note that because Blender does not support importing FBX models, you might want to use the FBX converter tool (see below) to convert to COLLADA or export directly to COLLADA. As before, use Z up and include animations if your model needs them. Since Blender is right-handed and uses Z up like 3ds Max, the default Y Forward setting also should be used.

Figure 3-6. *Exporting FBX models in Blender*

Other Formats and Exporting from Other Tools

Like Blender, many other tools (LightWave, CINEMA 4D Studio, etc.) support FBX and COLLADA exporting well too, but might be less powerful as a shader rendering preview tool. While Blender and 3ds Max use Z as the up axis, most other tools use Y, so the same export settings as in Maya can be used there.

OBJ is also often used as the common exchange format for static geometry, but it does not contain material or animation data, making it less useful for directly importing into games, or at least requiring you to set up material and shader parameters in the game engine or editor. For some tools, like the popular ZBrush sculpting tool, this limitation does not matter because they focus on creating static geometry. The Delta Engine supports importing from FBX, COLLADA (.dae), OBJ, 3ds, and DXF files, and you can use the free FBX converter from Autodesk[3] to convert among these formats.

There are also cases where it makes sense to use a specific 3D package format (e.g., .max from 3ds Max or .mb from Maya) if you need specific features not available in exported file formats. There is, however, a considerable amount of work required to support those file formats, and we do not recommend them at all. If you really want to work directly with 3ds Max or Maya data, use the built-in scripting abilities and export exactly what you need in your own format.

In addition to the FBX and COLLADA file formats, which we'll discuss in the next two sections, the following 3D formats are pretty common for games and in general:

- .mb: Maya binary file extension, used for Maya only

- .ma: Maya ASCII files, which can be edited with a text editor

- .max: Default extension for 3ds Max

- .obj: The object file format is a simple data format which contains 3D geometry exclusively

- .ase: The ASCII file format, mostly coming from 3ds Max

- .3ds: Obsolete 3ds Max format dating from DOS times

- .dxf and .dwg: Autocat file extensions

- .w3d: Shockwave scene export extension

- .blend: Native format for Blender; not used much

- .X: DirectX-specific file format, also sometimes used with XNA. Outdated and not very good for animations

- .ms3d: MilkShape 3D low-polygon modeling format, mostly used for Half-Life games and mods

- .b3d: Blitz3D engine file format, used by the Blitz3D programming language and its games

- .dts or .dsq: Torque engine 3D format; not used much

FBX SDK

We have talked a lot about file formats and how to export or convert 3D models, but how do you get those files into your game? You could try to write your own importer, which is actually not that hard for many simpler formats (.ase, .obj) and also possible for COLLADA (see next section) because you can extract only the data you actually need. However, to fully support advanced formats and stay up to date with the latest tools, it is a much better idea to use an existing engine or library, which can be integrated into your workflow. We decided to use the FBX SDK in addition to COLLADA in the Delta Engine to support a number of different 3D formats coming from different tools.

---

[3]Autodesk. "FBX Plug-Ins, Converter, and QuickTime Viewer Downloads." http://usa.autodesk.com/adsk/servlet/pc/item?id=10775855&siteID=123112.

In case you do not have any 3D content creation tools installed and you just want to check out some FBX files, you can use the FBX QuickTime plug-in from Autodesk to look at FBX files (see Figure 3-7).

Figure 3-7. *Using the QuickTime FBX plug-in to check out 3D models*

The FBX SDK (the current version is 2014.1[4]) is very complex and outside of the scope of this article. Sadly, the SDK is also only available for C++ and Python, which makes it a bit harder for .NET developers or other language users to use. If you are working with the XNA content pipeline, you can use the FBX content importer directly, but you won't have much control over it.

Alternatively, you can write a little tool to convert FBX files into your own format or write a library using the FBX SDK for your content pipeline. If all you need is to convert from one format to another (e.g., from FBX to COLLADA if you only want to support COLLADA directly), you can also use the FBX converter tool, which comes in both a GUI and a command-line version, making conversions among FBX, COLLADA, 3ds, DXF, and OBJ easy (see Figure 3-8).

---

[4]Autodesk. "3D Data Interchange Technology." http://usa.autodesk.com/fbx/.

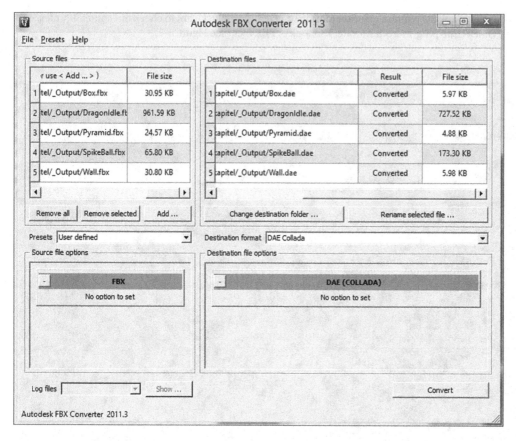

Figure 3-8. *The FBX Converter can be used to convert among FBX, COLLADA, 3DS, OBJ, and DXF*

If you use an engine supporting FBX files, it will most likely use the FBX SDK as well. There are many samples in the SDK, and if you keep your feature set to a minimum, you can get to the 3D data very quickly. However, the more features you want to support, the more you have to fight with the SDK, strange naming, and other issues, which is certainly not much fun for non-C++ programmers.

COLLADA Document Format

The COLLADA document format uses the extension .dae (digital asset exchange) and is basically just an XML file describing the 3D scene (see Figure 3-9 for an example). It is very extensible because each developer can add and extract his own nodes easily into existing files. As with any scene graph-based format, you choose to ignore unsupported nodes, but in our opinion the COLLADA format makes it much easier to extract useful information and ignore the rest. There are also tons of open source libraries, tools, and plug-ins available, which made this format very popular five years ago. COLLADA files are also supported by most engines and 3D tools. However, the format is not as widely used in games anymore because Autodesk has pushed their FBX format, and most game engines and frameworks support FBX files better than COLLADA.

```
1   <?xml version="1.0" encoding="utf-8"?>
2   <COLLADA xmlns="http://www.collada.org/2005/11/COLLADASchema" version="1.4.0">
3     <asset>
4       <contributor>
5         <author></author>
6         <authoring_tool>FBX COLLADA exporter</authoring_tool>
7         <comments></comments>
8       </contributor>
9       <created>2012-04-15T10:41:27Z</created>
10      <modified>2012-04-15T10:41:27Z</modified>
11      <revision></revision>
12      <title></title>
13      <subject></subject>
14      <keywords></keywords>
15      <unit meter="0.010000"/>
16      <up_axis>Z_UP</up_axis>
17    </asset>
18    <library_materials>
19      <material id="hlslShader1" name="hlslShader1">
20        <instance_effect url="#hlslShader1-fx"/>
21      </material>
22    </library_materials>
23    <library_effects>
44    </library_effects>
45    <library_geometries>
46      <geometry id="pPyramid1-lib" name="pPyramid1Mesh">
47        <mesh>
48          <source id="pPyramid1-lib-Position">
49            <float_array id="pPyramid1-lib-Position-array" count="15">
50  0.000002 -6.112185 -12.224371
51  -12.224371 -6.112185 -0.000001
52  -0.000001 -6.112185 12.224371
53  12.224371 -6.112185 0.000000
54  0.000000 6.112186 0.000000
55  </float array>
```

Figure 3-9. *Sample COLLADA file. The format allows figuring out most things just by reading it*

For example, the XNA content pipeline supports only FBX files and the outdated X file format. If you still want to import COLLADA files, there are several libraries and samples available. One of the authors, Benjamin Nitschke, wrote a comprehensive article in early 2007 on how to import "Skeletal Bone Animations and use Skinning with COLLADA Models in XNA."[5]

COLLADA files still work great, and when you don't want to include shader parameters from 3ds Max or Maya, which are always tricky, you need specific COLLADA plug-ins, but those are no longer supported in the latest Max or Maya versions. Static geometry can easily be handled with COLLADA, and all animation data works great out of the box. In addition, you can extend the format to include your own XML nodes anywhere in the XML tree.

---

[5]exDream. "Skeletal Bone Animation and Skinning with Collada Models in XNA." http://exdream.com/Blog/post/2007/02/25/ Skeletal-Bone-Animation-and-Skinning-with-Collada-Models-in-XNA.aspx.

Critics say the COLLADA format is a bit verbose and is bigger than binary file formats, but the whole purpose of COLLADA is to provide an exchange format, which also works great for importing 3D data into game engines. You should obviously include only the data you actually need in your game. It does not make much sense to include 100MB COLLADA or 3ds Max level files if all you need is a few hundred kilobytes of real level data. See the "Optimizing for Mobile Devices" section of this chapter for details on making imported 3D data as small as possible.

Models for Labyrinth

As described at the beginning of this chapter, the game Labyrinth consists of just four 3D models (see Figure 3-10):

- Dragon with animations
- Spikeball
- Wall
- Box

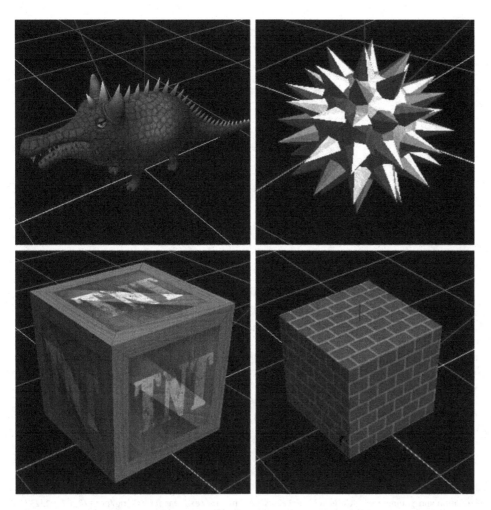

Figure 3-10. *3D Models for the sample game Labyrinth*

Normally, polygon count, shader complexity, fillrate, and the target platform should be considered when creating 3D content, but in our case none of these is an issue because

- The models are either very simple or were created with a low polygon limit in mind.

- Textures are small (256 x 256, 512 x 512), opaque, and can be combined. The fillrate is also not an issue because everything is opaque and almost no overdraw occurs.

- The pixel shader currently consists of just two instructions (multiplying the diffuse map color with the lighting).

- All content runs fine on the target platforms. The engine optimizations (see next section) also help.

Normally you should be a little more aware of texture sizes, reducing shader complexity, and removing unused content. One of the most challenging problems for artists is finding the right balance for texture sizes; you want to make everything look the best it can while still staying within platform limits. Optimizing a complex 3D game for mobile platforms can be a very hard task. The earlier you start profiling and making sure you don't add too many complex rendering features, the easier it becomes to keep high frame rates in your game.

As we worked on this chapter and the sample game, most of our time was spent fighting with exporting issues (missing normals, shader parameters, different issues exporting from different programs—all that fun) and programming the actual importing and rendering. As the engine developers, we obviously spent more time than a game development team would; those programmers can use existing engines or tools and simply agree on using 3D content creation programs that work for them.

However, having control over the import process can be a huge advantage for optimizations, and thanks to that, atlas generation and UV remapping (see Figure 3-11) can be accomplished easily with the Delta Engine. UV remapping is a technique usually performed manually by artists. It involves combining several meshes into a bigger one and merging the original textures into a bigger atlas texture. One caveat: tiling is usually not possible, so we added an extra flag to exclude tiled textures. It makes sense to fine-tune this process manually, but it can get very complicated when building for different platforms with different texture sizes and shaders, thus we tried to automate it in the Delta Engine. This allowed us to optimize for mobile platforms, leaving out features and texture maps that would be too slow (e.g., normal mapping, specular mapping, etc.).

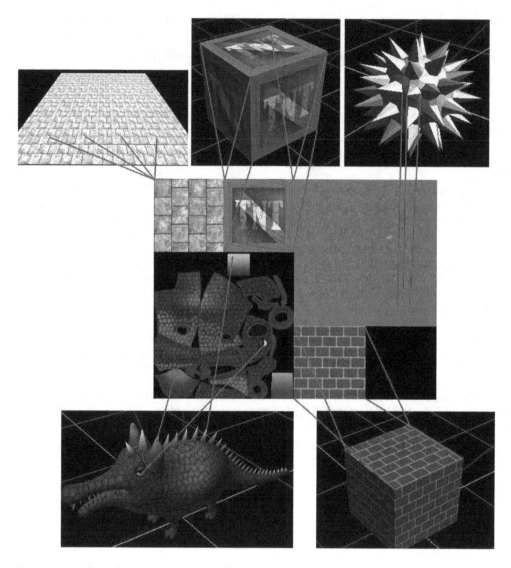

Figure 3-11. *The Delta Engine automatically merges images into atlas textures and remaps UVs*

Importing into the Delta Engine

Once we were done figuring out all the differences and issues between different exported models and formats, it was time to import all models for use in the Labyrinth game. In the Delta Engine,):this is done with the ContentManager tool (see Figure 3-12). All you have to do is to create a content project and drag and drop files you want to be used into your project. The imported content is then converted to optimized native file formats (e.g., images will become .dds, .etc, or .pvr textures depending on the platform). For the imported FBX models, all unneeded data is stripped out and just the vertices and indices are stored. In the Labyrinth game, each vertex of all the 3D meshes just uses a position, a normal vector, and the UV coordinates. All vertices sharing the same data are also merged and referenced via the indices array. In addition, vertex data is compressed for mobile platforms using 8-bit and 16-bit values instead of full 32-bit float values (see the next section for more information).

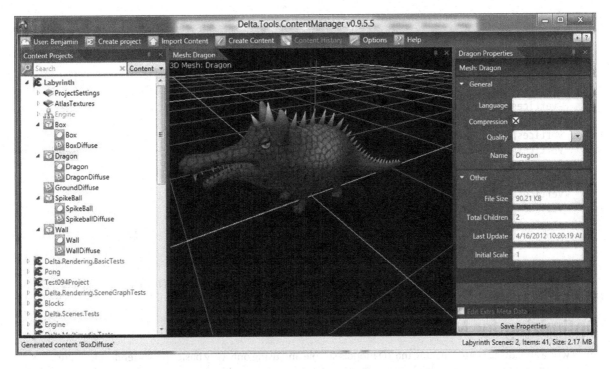

Figure 3-12. *Importing and checking 3D content with the Delta Engine ContentManager*

For the Labyrinth game, currently just the following content is used:

- An extra GroundDiffuse texture for the ground plane

- The Box, Dragon, Spikeball, and Wall meshes each with their material data and used diffuse map texture

Because we tested the different FBX exporters of 3ds Max, Maya, and Blender, the 3D models have different up axis setup. It is important to note that even when exporting an FBX file with Z up, the 3D data will be saved in the original format (e.g., with Y up when it comes from Maya). In order to fix that, we used a little helper method (see Listing 3-1 for some sample code) to convert all vertices and normals by switching Y and Z around and then negating Z. This works okay for static geometry, but it might cause problems for more complex geometry and animations. These issues can be fixed as well, but more testing and tweaking is usually required.

Listing 3-1. A Helper Method for Converting Vertices and Normals when Exporting an FBX File

```
/// <summary>
/// In case the scene was created with Y-Up originally
/// we need to convert it to Z-Up space by switching Y and Z
/// around and negating Z.
/// </summary>
public static void ConvertYUpAxisToZUpAxis(
  ComplexVertex[] vertices)
```

```
{
  for (int i = 0; i < vertices.Length; i++)
  {
    vertices[i].Position = new Vector(
      vertices[i].Position.X,
      vertices[i].Position.Z,
      -vertices[i].Position.Y);
    vertices[i].Normal = new Vector(
      vertices[i].Normal.X,
      vertices[i].Normal.Z,
      -vertices[i].Normal.Y);
    vertices[i].Tangent = new Vector(
      vertices[i].Tangent.X,
      vertices[i].Tangent.Z,
      -vertices[i].Tangent.Y);
  }
}
```

Check http://deltaengine.net/games/starterkits for the most recent version of the Labyrinth game.

Optimizing for Mobile Devices

Since we've already discussed making the 3D models simple and using only very basic shader rendering features, additional optimizations for mobile platforms are not really a big issue for this simple game. However, if your game becomes more intricate and you are using a lot of complex shaders and tons of high-polygon 3D models, you will run into performance problems very quickly. Not only do mobile devices render much more slowly than powerful GPUs on the PC, but they range from totally outdated and poor performance (iPhone 3G, OpenGL ES 11, older Android devices) to pretty decent performance (iPad 3, huge resolution, or PS Vita).

Obviously, trying to optimize all important aspects will help achieve good rendering performance, but more than anything you should constantly check to see if everything is still running smoothly or if you need to spend more time reducing content and doing some optimizations yourself. For example, the ContentManager of the Delta Engine will optimize vertex formats and shaders for you based on your settings, but it will not simplify the overall complexity of your game. This task is left to the game designer. He has to decide which features are crucial and which can be left out. If you are using complex 3D models with lots of polygons on PCs or consoles, it makes a lot of sense to reduce them drastically for mobile devices (level of detail (LOD) for 3D models is nothing new).

As you can see in Figure 3-13, lots of little tweaks and optimizations can be made for each mobile platform. In our opinion, most of these settings only have to be established (or at least accepted by everyone) once at the beginning of a project. It will be hard to convince artists who have worked on PC or console games to limit their creations to those rules. For example, many artists will argue that 36 bones for an animated model are not enough. The Dragon in the sample game originally had 40 bones, but we deleted a few and got the number below 36. The limit is not really 36 bones (depending on the platform, you could go up to 80 or 240), but keeping most models below the limits helps performance. Another important setting for animated models is the number of vertex influences each bone can have and the fps limit for animations. On a PC, you might allow four influences per bone and save up to 30 or even 60 fps of animation data, which can easily result in a megabyte less per animation. Consider the following:

- 80 bones
- 30 fps for the animation data

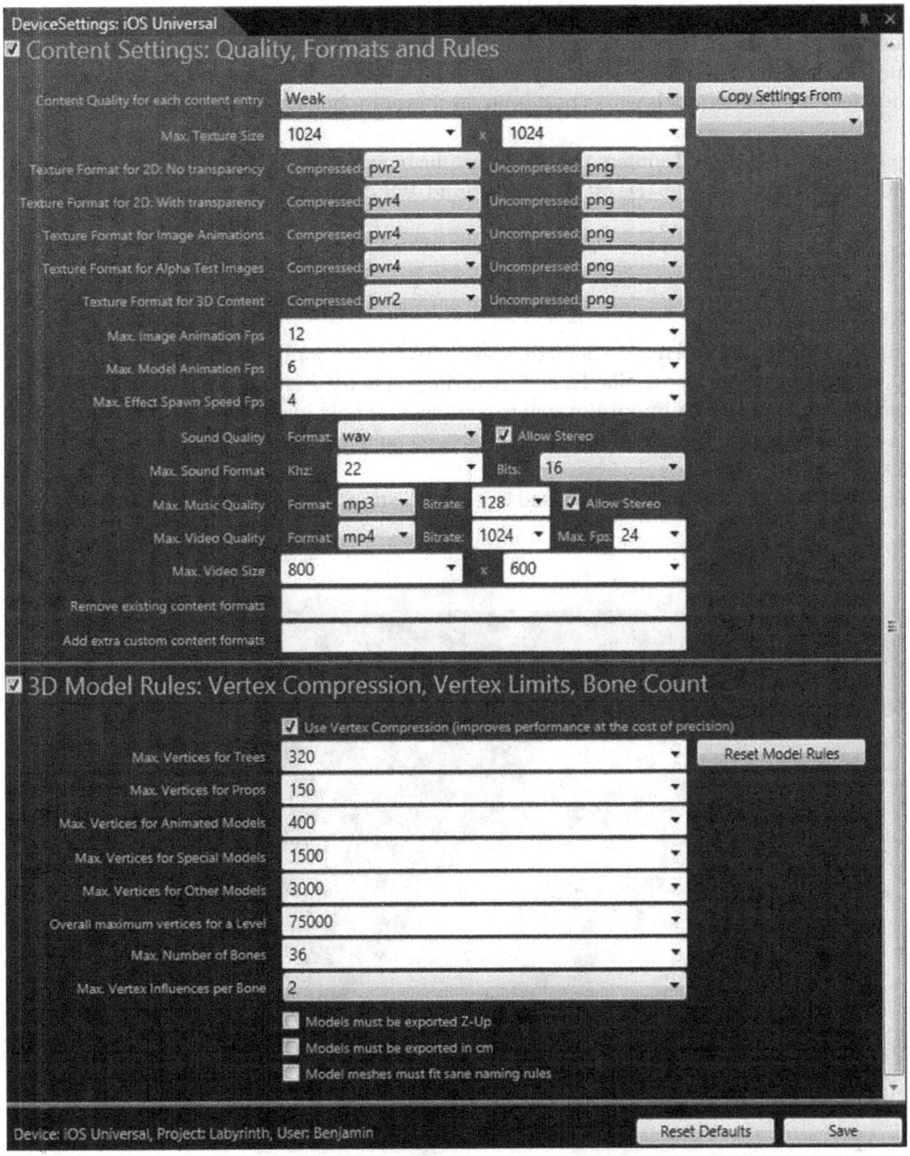

Figure 3-13. *iOS content settings for the Labyrinth content project*

Storing 30*80 matrices per second would result in 30*80*16*4 bytes = 150 kB, so at 6–7 seconds, a megabyte of animation data is needed. If we can get away with 36 bones, just 6 fps, and storing 12 values per animation matrix, this figure decreases to 6*36*12*4 bytes = 10 kB. Obviously, if the animations do not look good with less data, you need to increase the fps. In most projects, we have either saved enough pre-calculated animation matrices to look good enough, or we stored only the bare minimum and used blending between the animation matrices at the cost of a few CPU cycles to save a lot of memory.

All the other limits, like the maximum number of vertices for different model groups, also depend very much on your game. If you just show a single 3D model in the center of the screen, you can obviously allow a much higher polygon count than in a game with hundreds of meshes showing at the same time. We have found that a good mix of pre-merged level meshes and a few animated models works best even on slower mobile devices for our mobile RPG game Soulcraft.

You can download the project source code and content yourself or get the binaries[6] to see the game on PC or mobile platforms. We tested and used the engine on PC, Web (HTML5), iOS, Android, Windows 8, and Windows Phone 8.

Final Tips

You can check out the Labyrinth sample game and the Delta Engine on our web site.[7] Source code for this game, other tutorials and sample games, and the engine are also available, and we invite you to try them out for yourself. If you have questions about the game, the engine, or FBX importing, you can also ask for help in our forums. The point of this example is not to show a complete game, but instead to provide a starting point for anyone interested in writing his own multiplatform games in .NET.

The level displayed in Figure 3-14 is just a simple ASCII-based level (see Listing 3-2) rendered out, which takes less than 20 lines of code.

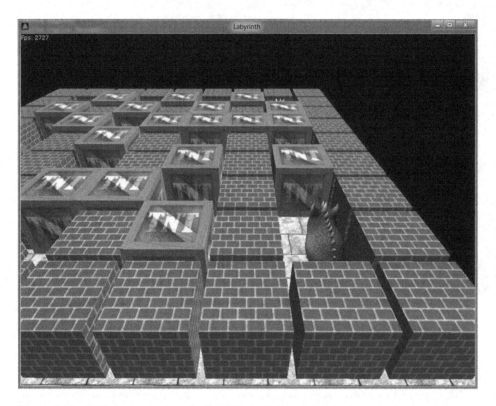

Figure 3-14. Early in-game screenshot of the Labyrinth game

---

[6]Delta Engine. "Labyrinth 3D example game." http://deltaengine.net/games/starterkits#labyrinth.
[7]Delta Engine. http://deltaengine.net/.

Listing 3-2. The 9 x 9 Area in the Level

```
// W: Wall, B: Box, X: Wall+Box, D: Dragon, S: Spikeball, G: Goal
private char[,] level = new char[,]
{
  { 'W', 'W', 'W', 'W', 'W', 'W', 'W', 'W', 'W', },
  { 'W', 'D', 'W', 'X', 'W', ' ', 'W', 'G', 'W', },
  { 'W', ' ', 'W', ' ', 'B', 'B', 'W', ' ', 'W', },
  { 'W', 'B', 'W', 'B', 'W', ' ', 'W', 'B', 'W', },
  { 'W', ' ', 'W', ' ', 'W', 'B', 'W', ' ', 'W', },
  { 'W', 'B', 'B', 'B', 'B', ' ', 'B', ' ', 'W', },
  { 'W', 'X', 'W', 'X', 'W', 'X', 'W', 'B', 'W', },
  { 'W', 'S', 'B', ' ', 'B', ' ', 'B', ' ', 'W', },
  { 'W', 'W', 'W', 'W', 'W', 'W', 'W', 'W', 'W', },
};
```

Conclusion

Using any format for static geometry is supported well in most tools and engines. Converting among formats (FBX, DAE, 3ds, OBJ, DXF, etc.) is also possible, especially if you don't care about advanced features like shader parameters. However, with animation data, things get a bit more complex, and it makes sense to choose one format (e.g., FBX or COLLADA) and one 3D content creation tool with specific settings (e.g., Z up, 1 unit = 1 cm) and stick with it. We have had positive experience with FBX, which works great for static and animated geometry and is supported by most tools and engines nowadays. If you need a little bit more flexibility or want to write your own 3D loader, COLLADA might be an easier choice for you.

CHAPTER 4

■ ■ ■

Building Procedural Geometry Using MAXScript (Voronoi Polygons)

Alessandro Ardolino

Procedural geometry modeling is a smart solution for some tasks that are tedious from an artist's perspective, or as sometimes happens, for a task that simply cannot be accomplished within a given production schedule. For example, consider the task of building a complex set of shapes such as broken glass. For an artist, this modeling task would be very time-consuming. A better solution might be to automate the process of building all the glass pieces while retaining the old shape.

This chapter explains how to do just that using a technique that can be adapted to solve a wide variety of problems. I will illustrate a way to create a complex polygon pattern using the powerful scripting tools provided by 3ds Max. This versatile pattern is known as a Voronoi diagram[1], named after Georgy Voronoy[2], the Ukrainian mathematician who defined it.

Please refer to the Wikipedia article for the formal definition of the diagram. For our purpose it will be defined as

Let P represent a set of sites p(x, y) in a 2D space: for each p in P, the Voronoi cell V(p) (or the Voronoi polygon) is the region that contains all the points closer to p than all the other sites in P.

Using terms more common in the CG world, given a set of vertices in a 2D space, a Voronoi polygon is the one built around a vertex including all of the 2D space closer to it than the other vertices. Figure 4-1 shows a common Voronoi diagram.

---

[1]"Voronoi diagram." http://en.wikipedia.org/wiki/Voronoi_diagram.
[2]"Georgy Voronoy." http://en.wikipedia.org/wiki/Georgy_Voronoy.

Figure 4-1. *A Voronoi diagram*

In nature, the Voronoi diagram can be seen on a turtle's carapace, a giraffe's skin, the cracks in dried mud, and much more. There are many applications of this pattern in the CGI field, from procedural texture creations to fracturing object simulations.

MAXScript and the Sample Code

MAXScript, the built-in scripting language for Autodesk 3ds Max, provides a number of methods to interact with mesh nodes. These are contained in the `meshOp` struct, and in the sample code they are used to get/set information from/to the meshes. The `snapshotAsMesh` command returns a mesh copy of the argument; in my example, it will be used both for performance and for practical matters. MAXScript works faster with Editable Meshes than Editable Polys; another advantage of Editable Meshes is that they provide access to the explicit triangles of the object. To improve the performance of the script, the `suspendEditing()` and `resumeEditing()` methods, which disable the Modify Panel interface during execution, will be used. In MAXScript, custom-generated meshes are created using the `mesh()` command with two arrays as its arguments: an array of vertices and an array of faces.

Voronoi and Delaunay

To generate a Voronoi diagram, the sample code uses a property of the Delaunay triangulation. Given a set of vertices, P, it's a Delaunay triangulation, DT(P), if no point of this set is inside the circumcircle[3] of any triangle of DT(P). Figures 4-2 through 4-4 illustrate this process (source: `en.wikipedia.org/wiki/Delaunay_triangulation`).

---

[3]"Circumscribed circle." `http://en.wikipedia.org/wiki/Circumscribed_circle`.

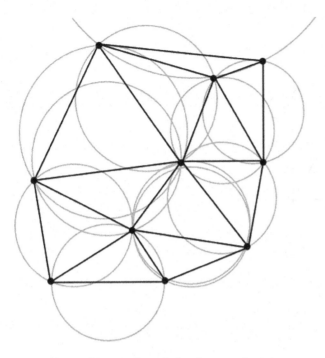

Figure 4-2. *Delaunay triangulation for a set of points*

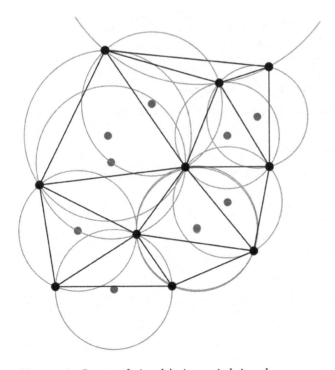

Figure 4-3. *Centers of triangle's circumcircle in red*

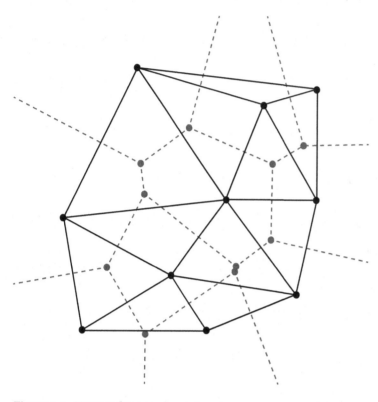

Figure 4-4. *Voronoi diagram drawn in red*

The Voronoi diagram is created by connecting all the centers of the triangle's circumcircles sharing the same vertex obtained during the Delaunay triangulation. Further information about Voronoi diagram building and the Delaunay triangulation is available in the references section.

The rest of this chapter illustrates how to build the Voronoi diagram. I will demonstrate

- How to populate an existing mesh with more vertices to create random set of points to triangulate.

- An algorithm to compute the triangulation of the point set.

- How to build the Voronoi diagram connecting the centers of the circumcircles of every triangle in the Delaunay mesh.

Figure 4-5 illustrates these steps.

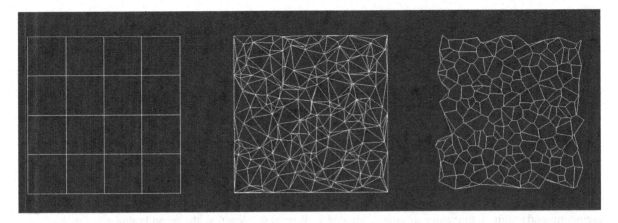

Figure 4-5. *From left to right, the base mesh, the Delaunay triangulation mesh, and the resulting Voronoi diagram*

What the Script Does

The script you are going to build will be composed of three main procedures and some utility functions:

- fn_delaunayTriangulation is the procedure used to create a random point distribution over the XY plane, or, if a mesh is passed as an argument, inside its triangles using barycentric coordinates. This function will return a triangulated mesh.

- fn_voronoiDiagram is the procedure used to derive the Voronoi diagram using the triangulated Delaunay mesh.

- ut_compareAngle is a utility procedure used to find the right order in which to build each Voronoi polygon.

- ut_compareVx is used to order the vertex array along the X axis.

- ut_isTriangleContained checks to see if a triangle is inside the Delaunay triangle array yet or needs to be added.

- ut_isInsideCircumcircle checks to see if a vertex is inside a triangle's circumcircle.

Two simple data structures will be defined to help the computation:

- struct triangle(p1,p2,p3) to store triangle data

- struct tEdge(p1,p2) to store edge data during the swapping stage in the Delaunay triangulation

The Code: Utility Functions and Data Structures

The Voronoi diagram computation code is based on two main procedures, one for the Delaunay triangulation and one to achieve your diagram. But to get more readable and practical code, you need some utility procedures and data structures. Two very simple data structures are used in the code, one storing a single triangle and one for the triangle's edges:

- struct triangle (p1,p2,p3) defines a triangle

- struct tEdge (p1,p2) defines an edge, used to mark the triangle's edge to split

These structs will be used in the next procedures as array elements. The p1..p3 variables will contain vertices in 2D or 3D spaces. They are needed to store information about the triangle's edges to find the right ones to swap or delete from the Delaunay triangulation mesh.

```
fn ut_compareAngle v1 v2 =
(
  if(v1.z < v2.z) then return -1
  else return 1
)
```

The function ut_compareAngle will be used to compare the angles between the Voronoi cell center and its surrounding vertices to find the right order to get a proper convex polygon. MAXScript lets the user define his own compare function to sort arrays containing complex elements. According to the MAXScript documentation, the qsort command takes the array and a comparison function as input. This comparison procedure will take two values as arguments and return 0 if the values are equivalent, -1 if the first value is less than the second value, and 1 in the other case.

```
fn ut_compareVx v1 v2 =
(
  if(v1.x < v2.x) then return -1
else if(v1.x > v2.x) then return 1
  else return 0
)
```

The ut_compareVx procedure will be used to compare two vertices and order their array along X axis values.

```
fn ut_isInsideCircumcircle p t &circumCircle =
(
  --check for the coincidence
  if( abs(t.p1.y - t.p2.y) == 0 and abs(t.p2.y - t.p3.y) == 0 ) then
  (
    print("error, coincidence\n");
    return false
  )

  if(abs(t.p2.y - t.p1.y) == 0) then
  (
    m2 = -(t.p3.x - t.p2.x) / (t.p3.y - t.p2.y)
    mx2 = (t.p2.x + t.p3.x) / 2.0
    my2 = (t.p2.y + t.p3.y) / 2.0
    circumCircle.x = (t.p2.x + t.p1.x) / 2.0
    circumCircle.y = m2 * (circumCircle.x - mx2) + my2
  )
  else if ( abs(t.p3.y-t.p2.y) == 0 ) then
  (
    m1 = - (t.p2.x-t.p1.x) / (t.p2.y-t.p1.y)
    mx1 = (t.p1.x + t.p2.x) / 2.0
    my1 = (t.p1.y + t.p2.y) / 2.0
    circumCircle.x = (t.p3.x + t.p2.x) / 2.0
    circumCircle.y = m1 * (circumCircle.x - mx1) + my1
  )
```

```
else
(
  m1 = - (t.p2.x-t.p1.x) / (t.p2.y-t.p1.y)
  m2 = - (t.p3.x-t.p2.x) / (t.p3.y-t.p2.y)
  mx1 = (t.p1.x + t.p2.x) / 2.0
  mx2 = (t.p2.x + t.p3.x) / 2.0
  my1 = (t.p1.y + t.p2.y) / 2.0
  my2 = (t.p2.y + t.p3.y) / 2.0
  circumCircle.x = (m1 * mx1 - m2 * mx2 + my2 - my1) / (m1 - m2)
  circumCircle.y = m1 * (circumCircle.x - mx1) + my1
)

--check on distances and circumcircle radius
dx = t.p2.x - circumCircle.x
dy = t.p2.y - circumCircle.y
rsqr = dx*dx + dy*dy
circumCircle.z = sqrt(rsqr) --radius

dx = p.x - circumCircle.x
dy = p.y - circumCircle.y
drsqr = dx*dx + dy*dy      --point distance

if(drsqr <= rsqr) then return true
)
```

The ut_isInsideCircumcircle procedure checks to see if point p is inside the t triangle and stores the circumcircle attributes in the circumcircle variable. The & before a variable means that its value will be modified by the function. After a check for a degenerate triangle, the function finds the circumcircle for the current triangle, and using simple distance checks, discovers whether the passed vertex is inside or outside the circle. The circumcircle variable is a simple vector using its x and y components to store circumcircle center 2D coordinates and the z component to store the circumcircle radius. A degenerate triangle has collinear vertices; it is basically a segment.

The Code: the Delaunay Triangulation

This function starts from a mesh, and procedurally adding vertices inside its triangles (to get more interesting Delaunay meshes from simple objects) finds the triangulation solution; it uses the barycentric coordinate system to create more vertices inside a single triangle, expressing them based on an interpolation of the triangle's vertices coordinates. After generating the right set of vertices, a big triangle surrounding all the vertices is created, and vertex by vertex, a contain-check is performed. At this stage, new triangles are added to the Delaunay set and some are deleted, too.

For readability, I will examine the Delaunay triangulation function code in sections, starting with Listing 4-1.

Listing 4-1. The First Section of the Delaunay Triangulation Function Code

```
function fn_delaunayTriangulation vNumber baseMesh =
(
  --the triangles created during the triangulation
  local delunayTriangles = #()

  --contains the vertices to triangulate
  local vertices = #()
```

```
  --disable editing for speed
  suspendEditing()

  --mesh copy of the passed object
  customShapeMesh = snapshotAsMesh baseMesh

  --for every triangle in the mesh generate a random set of vertices inside it
  numFaces = meshop.getNumFaces customShapeMesh
  numVertices = meshop.getNumVerts customShapeMesh

  undo off
  (
    for i=1 to numFaces do
    (
      --get the coordinates of the three vertices
      triVertices = meshop.getVertsUsingFace customShapeMesh i
      vertexCoords = #()
      for j=1 to numVertices do
      (
        if(triVertices[j] == true) then
        (
          vertexCoords[(vertexCoords.count + 1)] = meshOP.getVert customShapeMesh j
        )
      )
      --generate some random points inside the triangle using barycentric coords
      for k = 1 to vNumber do
      (
        aa = random 0.0 1.0
        bb = random 0.0 1.0
        if(aa+bb > 1.0) then
        (
          aa = 1-aa
          bb = 1-bb
        )
        cc = 1.0 - aa - bb

        tempV = (aa * vertexCoords[1]) + (bb * vertexCoords[2]) + (cc*vertexCoords[3])
        append vertices tempV
      )
    )
    --append the customShapeMesh vertices too
    for j=1 to numVertices do
    (
      append vertices (meshOP.getVert customShapeMesh j)
    )
  )
------------------
-- continue below
------------------
```

The fn_delaunayTriangulation function takes two arguments. vNumber contains the number of new vertices that will be created inside each triangle of your existing geometry; baseMesh is the existing geometry. Please note that using a high value in vNumber could slow down the MAXScript computation time.

The barycentric coordinates are used to add vertices in triangles defined by the passed mesh: a point inside a triangle can be expressed in terms of triangle's vertices coordinates, using the following notation:

newVertex = a * tP1 + b * tP2 + c * tP3

a + b + c = 1.0

c = 1.0 - a - b

The sum of a, b, and c must be equal to 1, so generating a and b randomly (checking their sum, too), the c value will equal 1.0 minus a minus b.

At last, the vertices of the passed mesh will be added to your set, as in Listing 4-2.

Listing 4-2. The Vertices of the Passed Mesh Are Added to the Set.

```
--------------------
-- continue above
--------------------

--sort the vertex array over the x axis
  qsort vertices ut_compareVx

  --find the point plane bounds --> min MAX
  xmin = vertices[1].x
  ymin = vertices[1].y
  xmax = xmin
  ymax = ymin

  for p in vertices do
  (
    if(p.x < xmin) then xmin = p.x
    if(p.x > xmax) then xmax = p.x
    if(p.y < ymin) then ymin = p.y
    if(p.y > ymax) then ymax = p.y
  )

  dx = xmax - xmin
  dy = ymax - ymin

  if(dx > dy) then dmax = dx
  else dmax=dy

  xmid = (xmax + xmin) / 2.0
  ymid = (ymax + ymin) / 2.0

  --create the super triangle containing all the vertices in the array
  superTriangle = triangle [(xmid - 2*dmax), (ymid - dmax), 0.0] [xmid, (ymid + 2*dmax), 0.0]
[(xmid + 2*dmax), (ymid - dmax), 0.0]
  append delunayTriangles superTriangle
```

```
--include each vertex one at time and do triangulation
for p in vertices do
(
  --setup the edge buffer
  edges = #()

  --for all the triangles currently in the triangulated mesh, do the check
  for j = delunayTriangles.count to 1 by -1 do
  (
    t = delunayTriangles[j]
    circumCircle = [0,0,0]        --contains a circle using xy for the center and z for the radius

    --check if point p is inside the circumcircle of the current triangle
    inside = ut_isInsideCircumcircle p t circumCircle
    if(inside == true) then  --store the edges and delete the triangle from the triangulation
    (
      tedg = tedge t.p1 t.p2
      append edges tedg
      tedg = tedge t.p2 t.p3
      append edges tedg
      tedg = tedge t.p3 t.p1
      append edges tedg
      deleteItem delunayTriangles j
    )
  )

  --tag multiple edges to prevent their use when creating triangles
  for j=1 to edges.count do
  (
    e1 = edges[j]
    for k = j+1 to edges.count do
    (
      e2 = edges[k]
      if(e1.p1 == e2.p2 and e1.p2 == e2.p1) then
      (
        e1.p1 = [-1,-1]
        e1.p2 = [-1,-1]
        e2.p1 = [-1,-1]
        e2.p2 = [-1,-1]
      )
    )
  )

  --form new triangles using the remaining edges and current vertex
  for j=1 to edges.count do
  (
    ee = edges[j]
    if (ee.p1 == [-1,-1] or ee.p2 == [-1,-1]) then
      continue
```

```
        t = triangle ee.p1 ee.p2 p
        append delunayTriangles t
    )
  )


  --remove the supertriangle and its vertices
  for i=delunayTriangles.count to 1 by -1 do
  (
    t = delunayTriangles[i]
    if (t.p1 == superTriangle.p1 or t.p2 == superTriangle.p2 or t.p3 == superTriangle.p3 or
        t.p1 == superTriangle.p1 or t.p2 == superTriangle.p3 or t.p3 == superTriangle.p2 or
        t.p1 == superTriangle.p2 or t.p2 == superTriangle.p3 or t.p3 == superTriangle.p1 or
        t.p1 == superTriangle.p2 or t.p2 == superTriangle.p1 or t.p3 == superTriangle.p3 or
        t.p1 == superTriangle.p3 or t.p2 == superTriangle.p1 or t.p3 == superTriangle.p2 or
        t.p1 == superTriangle.p3 or t.p2 == superTriangle.p2 or t.p3 == superTriangle.p1
        ) then
        deleteItem delunayTriangles i
  )
-------------------
-- continue below
-------------------
```

Using the compare utility function, the vertex array is sorted along the X axis. Next, the bounding box of all the vertices is computed and a super-triangle surrounding the set of all the vertices is generated. One by one, all the vertices are compared to the triangles currently inside the triangulation set, and based on the inside-circumcircle check, new triangles are added or the existing ones are modified. At the end of this process, the super-triangle is deleted from the Delaunay set (see Listing 4-3).

Listing 4-3. The Final Delaunay Mesh

```
-------------------
-- continue above
-------------------
--create a mesh to see the results
  for t in delunayTriangles do
  (
    v=#()
    append v t.p1
    append v t.p2
    append v t.p3

    f=#([1,2,3])
    mm = mesh vertices:v faces:f
    mm.name = uniqueName "tri_000"
  )

  --select all the tri meshes and attach them to a void mesh
    delaunayMesh = editable_mesh()
    delaunayMesh.name = uniqueName "delaunayMesh_"
    deselect $*
    for i in $*tri_* do
      meshop.attach delaunayMesh i
```

```
    convertTo delaunayMesh PolyMeshObject
    polyop.weldVertsByThreshold delaunayMesh #{1..(delaunayMesh.GetNumVertices())}

  resumeEditing()
  return delaunayMesh
)
--end fn_delaunayTriangulation function
```

For every triangle in the Delaunay triangle array, a single mesh is created and later attached to a void mesh. The duplicated vertices are finally welded together. Figure 4-6 shows the base mesh and the results of the fn_delaunayTriangulation function. Notice how the triangles in the base mesh have been subdivided.

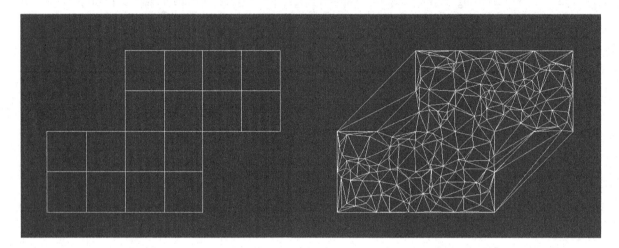

Figure 4-6. *Base mesh and Delaunay mesh*

The Code: the Voronoi Diagram

The Voronoi diagram procedure is pretty simple: it takes as arguments the triangulated Delaunay mesh, a numerical value used to delete Voronoi polygons of the same side amount, and the mesh used as the base for the triangulation. The base mesh is needed to cut out all the Voronoi polygons that lie outside it.

Every vertex in the triangulated mesh is a Voronoi cell center, and the centers of the triangles sharing the vertex are the cell vertices. So for every vertex in the triangulated mesh, you get all the faces that are sharing it, and for every face, you find the circumcircle center. The angle between the current vertex and the surrounding centers is calculated and stored in an array. This array will be ordered using a utility function. Finally, the new polygon is added to the Editable Poly object created in the first lines of the procedure (see Listing 4-4).

Listing 4-4. Creating the Voronoi Diagram

```
function fn_voronoiDiagram outTriMesh cutNgons baseMesh =
(
  --the object for the voronoi polys
  voronoiDiagram = editable_mesh()
  voronoiDiagram.name = uniqueName "voronoiPoly"
  convertTo voronoiDiagram PolyMeshObject
```

```
suspendEditing()

undo off
(
  numVertex = polyOp.getNumVerts outTriMesh
  for j = 1 to numVertex do
  (
    --for every face sharing the vertex
    faces = polyop.getFacesUsingVert outTriMesh j
    polyVertices = #() --vertices of the new face
    indexFace = #() --the face, contains vertices index...all the v[]
    for i = 1 to faces.count do
    (
      if faces[i] == true then
      (
        --get the face
        curF = polyOp.getFaceVerts outTriMesh i
        --find the center of the face and add to the polygon list
        x1 = (polyOp.getVert outTriMesh curF[1]).x
        x2 = (polyOp.getVert outTriMesh curF[2]).x
        x3 = (polyOp.getVert outTriMesh curF[3]).x
        y1 = (polyOp.getVert outTriMesh curF[1]).y
        y2 = (polyOp.getVert outTriMesh curF[2]).y
        y3 = (polyOp.getVert outTriMesh curF[3]).y

        D = 2*( x1*(y2 - y3) + x2*(y3 - y1) + x3*(y1 - y2))

        A = ( ((y1*y1 + x1*x1)*(y2 - y3)) + ((y2*y2 + x2*x2)*(y3 - y1)) + ((y3*y3 + x3*x3)*(y1 - y2)) )
        A = A / float(D)
        B = ( ((y1*y1 + x1*x1)*(x3 - x2)) + ((y2*y2 + x2*x2)*(x1 - x3)) + ((y3*y3 + x3*x3)*(x2 - x1)) )
        B = B / float(D)

        --check for the center, if it's inside the plane or inside the passed mesh it's ok
        if(baseMesh != "undefined") then
        (
          --check if the center is inside the triangles of the mesh using the barycentric coords
properties
          customShapeMesh = snapshotAsMesh baseMesh

          numFaces = meshop.getNumFaces customShapeMesh
          numVertices = meshop.getNumVerts customShapeMesh

          --for every triangle:
          for i=1 to numFaces do
          (
            --get the three vertices
            triVertices = meshop.getVertsUsingFace customShapeMesh i
```

```
            vertexCoords = #()
            for j=1 to numVertices do
            (
              if(triVertices[j] == true) then
              (
                vertexCoords[(vertexCoords.count + 1)] = meshOP.getVert customShapeMesh j
              )
            )

            --compute the vectors
            P = [A, B, 0]
            v0 = vertexCoords[3] - vertexCoords[1]
            v1 = vertexCoords[2] - vertexCoords[1]
            v2 = P - vertexCoords[1]

            --compute the dot products
            dot00 = dot v0 v0
            dot01 = dot v0 v1
            dot02 = dot v0 v2
            dot11 = dot v1 v1
            dot12 = dot v1 v2

            -- Compute barycentric coordinates
            invDenom = 1 / (dot00 * dot11 - dot01 * dot01)
            u = (dot11 * dot02 - dot01 * dot12) * invDenom
            v = (dot00 * dot12 - dot01 * dot02) * invDenom

            --Check if point is in triangle
            if (u > 0 and v > 0 and u + v < 1 ) then
            (
              append polyVertices [A, B,0]
              --exit --exit from the for loop
            )
          )
        )
      )
  )

  --find all the angles between the current vertex and all the voronoi vertices
  A = polyOp.getVert outTriMesh j
  for k = 1 to polyVertices.count do
  (
    --find the angle of B relative to A
    B = polyVertices[k] - A
    angl = (atan2 B.y B.x)
    polyVertices[k].z = angl
  )

  --sort using angle --> z value
  qsort polyVertices ut_compareAngle
```

```
    --restore the z value to zero, this value was previously used to store the angle value!
    for k = 1 to polyVertices.count do polyVertices[k].z = 0.0

    --should have quads polys and not ngons...
    indexVertex = #()
    for k=1 to polyVertices.count do
    (
      append indexVertex (polyOp.createVert voronoiDiagram polyVertices[k])
    )

    --check for triangle faces
    if(indexVertex.count > cutNgons) then
      polyop.createPolygon voronoiDiagram indexVertex
  )
)
resumeEditing()
return voronoiDiagram
)
```

To run the scripts and check the results on a base mesh, just execute the following code. The results should be similar to those shown in Figure 4-7. The mesh must be placed in the "top" view (y and x coordinates only).

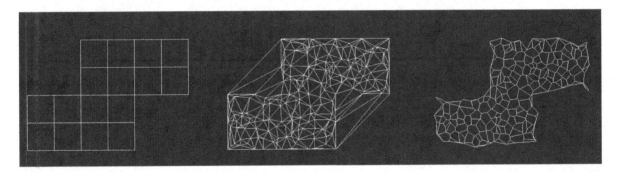

Figure 4-7. *Base mesh, Delaunay mesh, and Voronoi diagram*

```
baseMesh = $
outTriMesh = fn_delaunayTriangulation 8 baseMesh
fn_voronoiDiagram outTriMesh 2 baseMesh
```

Conclusion

This chapter offers an introduction to procedural geometry creation using the tools offered by MAXScript. The proposed Voronoi diagram computation code is basic and could be improved in a variety of ways. For example, the bounding edges of the base mesh are not considered or included in the resulting Voronoi diagram mesh. The code works only for planar base meshes and doesn't work in object space. The reader could improve it by removing the world space-only limitation and adding the base mesh boundary vertices to the Voronoi mesh to achieve the breaking surface effect.

■ ■ ■

## CHAPTER 5

A Uniform Geometry Workflow for Cutscenes and Animated Feature Films

Adrien Herubel, Venceslas Biri, Stepane Deverly, Antoine Galbrun

At DuranDuboi, as we started the preproduction of our first animated feature film in 2009 it became clear that our VFX production pipeline was no longer adequate. Instead of small, manageable projects involving a few generalists, we were now dealing with massive amounts of data requiring intense, short-term efforts from multiple teams of specialists. So with a relatively low budget, we focused on developing from scratch an efficient workflow for handling the massive amount of geometry produced by the different production departments.

But manipulating dynamic geometry is costly both in terms of computing power and storage. For example, the complex Autodesk Maya rigs on the main characters take nearly 60ms per frame to evaluate. In a typical shot, two or three of these characters will be present, making the sequence impossible to animate in real-time. Even worse, dynamic cloth and hair simulations can take up to a minute per frame to compute. Therefore, we decided that geometry should be precomputed or baked whenever possible.

Our key idea was to rely on a single geometry cache format tailored for efficient read, plugged into every software package we used, from modeling to compositing and rendering. Our ubiquitous cache system allowed us to design a set of tools for modification and visualization of the files. Those tools were used uniformly across the production pipeline and allowed us to reduce the usage of Maya, especially for automated geometry processing and quality control.

Moreover, this uniform geometry pipeline improved our workflow by allowing multiple departments to work simultaneously and reduced the overall computational and storage costs. As it turned out, we weren't the only ones thinking along these lines. Sony Pictures Imageworks simultaneously developed the basis of a similar solution, Alembic, which is an open interchange format focused on efficiently storing baked geometry (www.alembic.io). Alembic has now grown into a production-proven solution; it is stable and efficient enough to serve as the exchange format and API to implement the same pipeline as presented here. In this chapter, I will describe the four parts of our cache and show how it is integrated into our workflow.

Technology

Our cache system can roughly be divided into four parts: a low-level binary cache format, an I/O framework, commercial software plug-ins, and tools (see Figure 5-1).

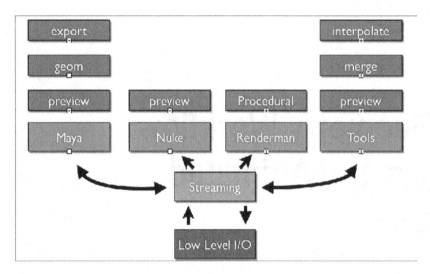

Figure 5-1. *The cache system software stack: low-level IO, streaming and serialization framework, software plug-ins, and tools*

Cache Format

The bootstrap section contains basic metadata and the header offset. Each header entry contains chunk metadata.

The cache file format is oriented towards two use cases: writing a huge quantity of geometry once, and reading parts of the geometry often. As the format is designed for writing in batches, it will be slightly inefficient in the case of multiple read-write cycles. However, in a production with a complex pipeline, this situation rarely occurs. Instead, each department produces caches for one department and uses cache from another, so the need for read-write caches is almost nonexistent.

Our files contain an arbitrary number of chunks. A chunk is an array of data, defined by a data type, a size, and a tag. A cache can be viewed as a general-purpose binary chunk dictionary. The binary layout on disk is shown in Figure 5-2. The bootstrap is a fixed-size header containing the API version number and an offset to the header. The chunks are written contiguously and an array of chunk metadata is stored, with each metadata cell containing a chunk offset, a size, a type, and a tag.

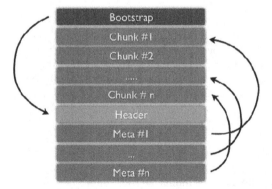

Figure 5-2. *Binary layout of our cache file format*

When a cache file is opened, the bootstrap is read to check for compatibility. Then using the header offset, the whole metadata array is read and transformed into a hash map. Chunks are read only on demand.

During the write process, chunks are immediately written to the disk, next to the last chunks of the cache, but metadata is kept in RAM. Metadata is stored only when all of the chunks have been written, and then the bootstrap section is updated with the header offset.

I/O Framework

On top of the low-level general-purpose cache format, we built a whole I/O framework capable of storing a full Maya scene in a cache file and streaming data from the cache to memory on demand.

We define an object as an independent component in a 3D scene such as a mesh, a group of hairs, or a particle system. Objects are split into several chunks referenced by a tag nomenclature. Atomicity is important for optimizing memory occupation depending on the use case; therefore a chunk contains only a small indivisible part of an object. The serialization and deserialization routines allow us to store and reconstruct any set of baked objects from the cache.

The basic I/O procedures can be used to access geometry directly, but for reading complete sets and shots, it is important to enforce strict memory occupation constraints. The framework contains a streaming component in charge of loading complete objects on demand and discarding the least recently used objects when memory occupation is too high.

Software Plug-ins

Our cache system is tightly integrated into most of the software packages used in production. The system is flexible enough so that the same cache file can be used for various use cases.

Cache Export

In our production pipeline, Autodesk Maya was used to produce final models and animations; therefore the cache export module was implemented as a Maya plug-in.

Any arbitrary scene hierarchy, or sub-part of a hierarchy, can be baked into a single cache file. We currently support mesh, nurbs, locators, particles, and fur geometry exported from the commercial software Joe Alter Shave and a Haircut. Objects are exported over an arbitrary number of frames into the same cache file. Static attributes, such as mesh topology, and UV coordinates are stored once. Potentially animated attributes such as transform matrices, deformed mesh vertex positions, and normals are stored for each frame.

As previously stated, objects are divided into numerous chunks. For example, the vertices of a mesh at a given frame n are stored in a separate chunk from those for topology, or normals, or UV coordinates. We also store bounding boxes and transforms separately.

Cache Preview

The cache preview offers real-time rendering of the geometry directly in the viewport and plays complex shots interactively. In this mode, the software has no knowledge of the geometry as it is exposed only as OpenGL proxies. Rendering is performed entirely in the plug-in and takes advantage of the streaming framework to load only what is needed to render. Whereas in this mode editing the geometry is impossible, it is faster to load, render, and play than classic Maya geometry and has a minimal memory footprint. Moreover, the on-demand nature of the frameworks enables us to expose only bounding boxes, or points (see Figure 5-3) to further reduce memory occupation on multi-gigabyte sets (see Figure 5-4). The preview mode is also available in The Foundry Nuke where it can be tremendously useful during compositing.

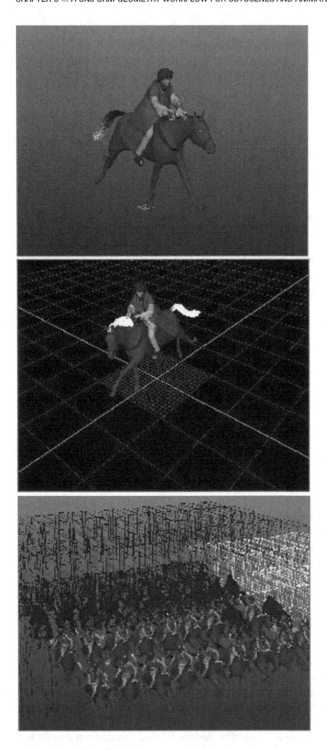

Figure 5-3. (*continued*)

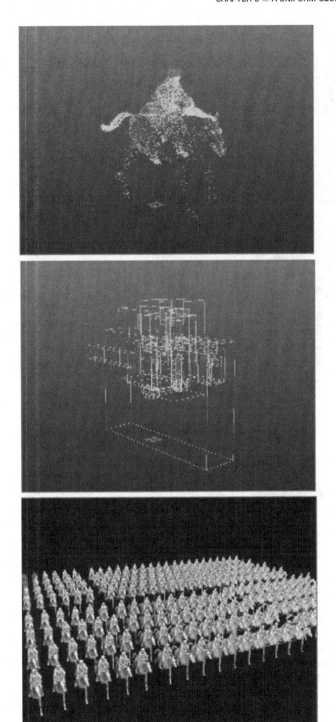

Figure 5-3. *Various cache usages for the 15K-polygon horseman model. From top: preview in Autodesk Maya, preview in The Foundry Nuke, instancing, point mode, bounding box mode, procedural in Pixar RenderMan*

Figure 5-4. *Screen captures of the Autodesk Maya viewport. The scene contains approximately 5M polygons and is displayed using various cache modes. We compare memory usage of cache display modes and Maya geometry. Measured on the City model, using a Core i7 920 2.67GHz, 16GB RAM, 7200tpm HDD, NVIDIA Quadro 4000*

Cache Geometry

When we need the geometry to be available in Maya for editing to solve collisions in physical simulations, we provide a cache geometry mode mimicking the geocache feature of Maya, but again, largely faster and with less memory overhead (see Figure 5-5). It involves injecting animated vertex data into an existing topology, making it available for editing and colliding in Maya. Later the edited geometry can be baked again and used as a preview.

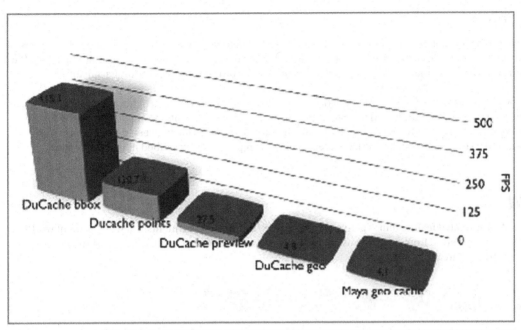

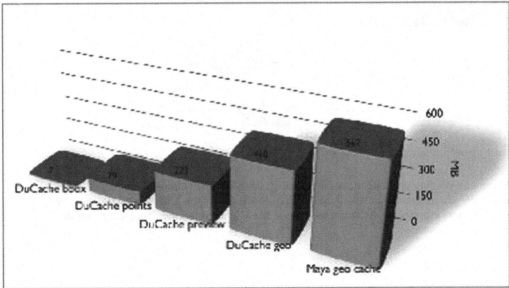

Figure 5-5. *Playback speed and memory usage for various cache modes against Maya Geometry Cache. Measured on the horseman model, using an Intel Core i7-920 2.67GHz, 16GB RAM, 7200tpm HDD, NVIDIA Quadro 4000*

Rendering Caches

The Pixar RenderMan interconnection is a fundamental building block in our uniform geometry pipeline, as a geometry cache can be used directly as a procedural primitive in RenderMan (see Figure 5-3), thus removing the need for geometry in RIB (RenderMan Interface Bytestream Protocol) files. Cache files are smaller and more flexible than RIB files. They can also be up to 10x faster to render than RIB files due to fast deserialization and coherent data layout.

Custom Tools

Finally, we developed a whole ecosystem around this cache format: real-time preview of multiple cache files, merging two cache files, quickly editing content of a chunk, adding interpolated frames, and even injecting additional data. We found that a homegrown system makes it easy to quickly create tools for processing geometric data, greatly enhancing our flexibility.

We found two tools particularly useful in production. First, the real-time preview in a lightweight visualizer was a real productivity gain for conformation and validation purposes. The visualizer could be opened directly from the asset manager and was much faster than using Maya to quickly validate data passing between departments. The merging tool was also a key component, as it enabled teams to work in parallel as described in the next section.

Workflow

The production of an animated feature film is generally divided into multiple departments. Each department works with specific input data, received from other teams, and specific output data, which is subsequently turned over to other departments (see Figure 5-6).

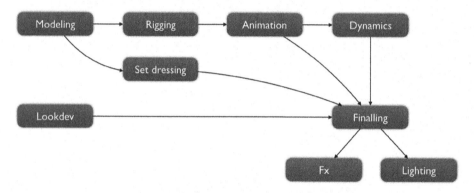

Figure 5-6. *Geometry asset production workflow*

Multiple departments produce geometry data, often for the same assets. This strong dependency chain is problematic, especially when retake requests are made. We tried to improve this process by systematically consolidating geometric data exported by departments in cache files. We also automated the merging of data produced in parallel for the same asset.

Our Pipeline

Great pipeline tools are tailored to production needs. Early specification of features and data models allows room for optimization and general efficiency.

Teams

As I mentioned at the beginning of this chapter, full-length films are characterized by high quality expectations and an enormous amount of produced data. Short animated films and small-length VFX productions can be handled entirely by a small team of generalists, but full-length productions call for multiple teams of specialists dedicated to the production of one stage or one particular type of asset.

As an example, our production teams were divided according to the following table. The numbers in Table 5-1 do not look high because they do not reflect the fact that most departments are not at their full size during the whole production time, allowing some artists to work across multiple departments.

Table 5-1. *DuranDuboi Animated Feature Film Preproduction Departments and Their Sizes*

Department	Approximate team size
Modeling	10
Rigging	5
Layout	10
Animation	40
FX	5
Texturing	10
Look development	10
Hair	5
Dynamics (Cloth)	5
Lighting	10
Compositing	10

Assets and Files

An asset is a logical entity which represents all the aspects of an atomic component across production stages. Asset types are generally production-specific or pipeline-specific. The most common are Characters, Sets, and Props. Under the name Asset are regrouped all the files, rules, or comments which define an asset, such as references, designs, Maya scenes, animation curves, or shading assignments.

In our pipeline, each of these files is defined by arbitrary properties such as the originating department or the quality setting. Each physical file belonging to this logical association is versioned so that each published version can be validated and each change can be reverted. For example, a Character could be composed of two base mesh files from the modeling department, one high-poly, and one low-poly; a hair model from the fur department; and a rigged model built by the rigging team. Each of those would be versioned separately. Each published file version is conserved and stored as a read-only file.

Artists generally work on "work in progress" files (or wip), which are not attached to a given asset but to an owner and team name. Versioning occurs when the artist publishes a file candidate for validation, generally using a dedicated pipeline tool. Upon publishing, the validation process begins, as well as the publish callbacks.

Each time a file is published or validated on the pipeline, a set of rules is automatically applied according to the file type, the nature of the validation, or the originating department. These callbacks accomplish a wide variety of tasks: validation requests, model merging, turntable generation, or automated conformation and tests. Thousands of these processes are executed each day and dynamically dispatched on the renderfarm. The ability to automate parts of our production pipeline was essential in the development of the geometry workflow.

Parallel Workflow

Our parallel pipeline (see Figure 5-7) automatically produces a cache containing baked geometry each time a new version of a model, an animation, or a simulation is published. Therefore each asset, animated or static, is available in form of a cache file.

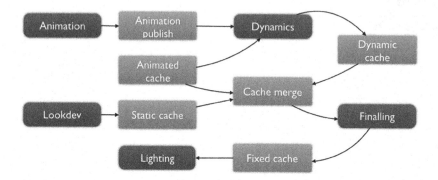

Figure 5-7. *Geometry asset production workflow using cache merging. Many departments can now work in parallel as merging is automated upon asset publication*

The main idea of a parallel workflow is to identify for each department what parts of the scene need to be editable in Maya and what parts can use baked data from caches. The layout team uses only the cache preview mode since they have no need to edit geometry, but must only populate shots with the needed assets. The animation department uses mixed-mode scenes, where animated characters are rigged, and where the set is either in a cache bounding box (which is a cache preview mode with only bounding boxes and matrices in memory) or in cache preview. The FX team in charge of fluid simulation needs partial geometry data for collision handling, so they use both the cache preview and cache geometry modes where necessary. Finally, the shading and lighting departments use only cache preview for shading assignment and light-rig construction.

Our pipeline allows the user to dynamically override the default settings and switch the cache mode of an asset, even back to plain old rigged geometry.

It is to be noted that our pipeline makes heavy use of the renderfarm for all baking and merging operations. The process is entirely transparent to the user, as baking and merging requests are asynchronously dispatched.

Merging

Multiple departments can induce the generation of baked geometry: modeling and texturing teams produce static geometry, cloth artists provide baked simulation, and animators create baked animation. One problem that can result from this workflow is that multiple teams might be working on different parts of the same model simultaneously. To address this problem, our pipeline enables this feature by automating the merging of cache files produced by multiple departments (see Figure 5-8). For example, a character cache in a lighting scene has UV coordinates and topology from the modeling department, animated shapes from the animation department, and animated clothes from the cloth department. If a modeler makes a retake on UV coordinates, a new cache is generated, then merged with previous animation and cloth caches, and finally updated in the lighting scene.

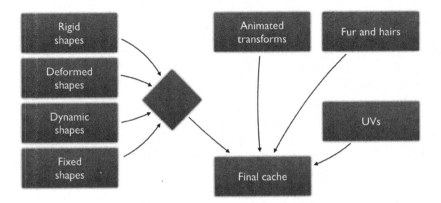

Figure 5-8. Each department produces different types of geometry data. Each time an asset is updated by a department, a cache is exported. Then the caches of various departments are merged together using a set of rules

Conclusion

At DuranDuboi, we developed a framework and a complete set of tools dedicated to the efficient handling of baked geometry in cache files. The system is used uniformly across all of our production pipelines. The ability to allow simultaneous work on the same models by different departments as well as the automated external processing of geometry data have proved extremely useful.

Our geometry production workflow is built to enable multiple teams of specialists to work in parallel. This solution is combined with our other tools such as the production tracker, asset versioning system, and job queue dispatcher. Such a system would remain equally efficient with an order of magnitude more people. Nevertheless, because this pipeline is aimed at tackling big production challenges, it is probably too constrained to suit small-scale teams of generalists.

Our uniform cache system reduces disk usage by consolidating final data into one file per asset and removing the need for geometry in RIB files. The cache preview and cache geometry modes in Autodesk Maya are faster and lighter than the alternatives. The main drawback of our system is the rigor imposed on users. As the systematical locking of various parts of the scene might appear daunting to artists, we addressed this issue by allowing them to switch back to plain geometry whenever needed.

The system has been used in production and will be upgraded. We expect future versions of the system to be able to support more commercial software programs such as VRay and Houdini. We know that the tag system for data chunks could benefit from increased flexibility and plan to address the issue. For example, each chunk should be referenced by more than one tag, and the chunk type metadata could be replaced by a tag. As geometry complexity is rapidly increasing, particular attention should be paid to memory management and out-of-core capabilities, notably using virtual memory mapping approaches such as presented in Kamp.[1]

---

[1] P.H. Kamp. "You're doing it wrong." Communications of the ACM 53:7 (2010), 55–59.

CHAPTER 6

■ ■ ■

Building a Rock-Solid Content Pipeline with the COLLADA Conformance Test Suite

Paula Berinstein and Rémi Arnaud

If there's one message emanating from the 3D content creation community these days, it's "Ouch!" We all know why. There's too much pain in the 3D content creation pipeline: incompatible formats, obsolescence of older material, platform limitations, and so on. Fortunately, there's something we can do to ease the pain: create tools that adhere to open standards, such as COLLADA, a royalty-free, open standard schema for exchanging 3D assets.

It's no wonder that the digital world is embracing openness. Digital citizens are realizing that the more proprietary their tools and formats, the more constrained they are, and the more money and time they have to spend in order to do their work. Often they find themselves recreating assets that already exist, just so they can exchange them with other team members or clients, or make them work with the latest version of their software. Tools and formats that use open standards enable them to be more productive and creative because components move effortlessly along the pipeline, freeing up creators to do what they do best: make cool stuff.

COLLADA, which is maintained by The Khronos Group, a nonprofit industry consortium, is defined by an XML namespace and schema that specify a list of features every COLLADA partner has agreed to support. The Khronos Group has devised a rigorous set of conformance tests for 3D tools that use COLLADA to help insure frictionless import and export operations. The tests have recently been open sourced and are now available at https://github.com/KhronosGroup/COLLADA-CTS.

Khronos wants to make it easy to achieve conformance, so they've devised two ways to license the tests. The **Adopters Package** is designed for vendors who want to be able to use Khronos technology logos and trademarks in their product marketing. The **Implementers Package** is aimed at developers and open source communities with more limited resources. Adopters pay a modest fee and get significant value: when your product passes the tests, you may submit the results to Khronos and earn the right to use the COLLADA trademarks and claim conformance. Your customers can buy your products with confidence, knowing that their output will be clean and easy to use with other tools. Implementers also get a great deal, but with limitations: you may download and use the tests for FREE, and, if you pass, use the "COLLADA™" *text* trademark, but you can't use the official COLLADA logo trademark or claim conformance. The Implementers Package is a great deal because you get a verified set of test cases and a testing framework that you can run as many times as you like in order to perform unit and regression testing—for nothing! If you had to write those tests yourself, you could spend thousands!

Membership in Khronos is not required in either case, but if you join, you get even more benefits, including access to all Khronos specifications and documentation, early access to the draft specifications, the ability to participate in work groups and the development of the specs and tests, discounted Adopter fees, and more.

Benefits of conformance include highly interoperable tools, credibility and good will, protection against product regression, easy-to-create use cases, streamlined procurement, clear customer expectations, and consistency of implementation with other vendors, not to mention happy and productive users.

In this chapter, which is based upon The Khronos Group's current COLLADA CTS Tutorial, we explain how to use the suite to build a rock-solid 3D content pipeline, saving a huge amount of time in the development of tools and games.

The tests may be used on one target application alone for both conformance and regression testing, or to verify interoperability between one application and another, such as Trimble SketchUp (formerly a Google product), Autodesk 3ds Max, and Autodesk Maya. There are 613 tests and three possible levels of conformance (badges)—Baseline, Superior, and Exemplary—but regardless of the application's capabilities, all the tests must be run. Based on the results, the framework determines which, if any, badge to award.

The conformance tests can be used on two types of applications: import only and import/export. Import-only applications include 3D document viewers, game engines, ray tracers, and rendering packages. Import/export applications include most traditional content creation tools that do modeling and animation. Both classes of applications must be able to render COLLADA data as an image because that is the primary method the CTS uses to determine whether a COLLADA document has been correctly understood. For a complete test, the software must also be able to import and export COLLADA documents. You can test applications that support only some of these functions, but they can only earn conformance within the context of a conformant implementation environment (i.e., one that has already passed the test suite) that provides the missing functionality.

The suite tests whether the target application does the following:

- Handles COLLADA input and output properly

- Renders files created under different conditions consistently

- Outputs COLLADA documents that conform to the COLLADA schema

Some of the issues tested are

- Completeness of support for each feature

- Robustness when bad data is encountered

- Appearance of images and movie clips

- Preservation of features during a load/save cycle

Types of tests include

- Minimal unit tests for specific features, like document referencing and skinning

- System tests that exercise desirable common scenarios, such as skinned rag doll export/import with COLLADA FX materials on different body parts

- Stress tests for very large scenes

- Handling of local or temporary test data

- Handling of invalid or corrupt data

All importers must be able to read any valid COLLADA document without failure, even if that document contains features not supported by the importer. Features beyond the importer's level of support are not required to be understood, but simply encountering them should not cause the importer to fail. Unusual or unexpected ordering or quantity of elements should not cause an importer to fail as long as the document validates to the schema. For example, library elements may occur in any order and libraries of the same type can appear multiple times. Importers must not require their own COLLADA extensions in order to understand valid documents.

All exporters must create documents that validate to the COLLADA schema. Documents exported by the implementation should support the same feature set as that implementation's importer in order to provide a lossless (roundtrip) content pipeline.

The CTS works through a GUI on computers running the Microsoft Windows operating system. You can also use a command-line interface, and certain functions can be performed through Windows Explorer.

Using the tests is a matter of installing, configuring, and running them. The broad steps are

- Prerequisites: Download and install the suite and some helper applications.

- Integration: Write and test a Python script.

- Set up the tests: Create a test procedure, add tests.

- Run the tests.

- Interpret the results.

- If you want to be able to use Khronos technology logos and trademarks on your products, submit results to Khronos. If you want to use the tests internally only, you don't need to submit results.

Things You Need to Know About the Tests

Before you start, there are a few concepts and ground rules you should know: the idea of "blessing," the types of tests the CTS presents, the fact that there are two cycles for each test, and where the input and output data reside.

Blessed Images

The CTS incorporates the idea of "blessing," which means that results have been officially "blessed" by Khronos, so they are considered correct and conformant by the COLLADA working group. A set of blessed images and animations—a control group to use as a baseline—comes with the test suite; you can compare these with your results to see how close you are and how you differ. Exact matches to the blessed images and animations are not required in order to pass. However, your application must generate images in a way that's internally consistent.

Types of Tests

There are three types of tests: simple, medium, and complex.

- **Simple**: Tests that pass/fail based on successful importing, or importing and then exporting a COLLADA document. Examples include tests that check for proper handling of URIs on import/export, checking for unwanted adding/removing of elements from the document, testing sensitivity to element ordering, and checking for the ability to process any valid COLLADA document without crashing.

- **Medium**: Tests that require a successful import, export, and rendering of the exported document in the target application. These tests are generally used to confirm that programs are correctly processing and re-exporting a document without corrupting the geometry and other elements in it.

- **Complex**: Like the medium tests, complex tests require a successful import, export, and rendering of the exported document in the target application. However, this type of test also insures that the application is correctly interpreting the contents of the document. It is used to check how well the application handles materials, textures, cameras, lights, etc.

Two Cycles

Each test runs through two cycles.

1. **The Export step**: The test case's COLLADA document is imported, rendered, and exported. This cycle tests whether the target application can import and work with a valid COLLADA document (that was possibly) created in another tool.

2. **The Validate step**: The COLLADA document that was exported in the first cycle is reimported into the target application, rerendered, and validated against the COLLADA schema. This cycle tests whether the document exported in the first cycle imports and compares properly and outputs valid COLLADA that can be imported by other conformant tools. The Validate step is needed to verify that the exported document meets criteria not tested in the Export step.

As you can see, a complete test includes two import and render operations. The first time, you import the test document furnished by Khronos; the second time, you import the document you just exported. The workflow is Import ➤ Render ➤ Export ➤ Import ➤ Render ➤ Validate.

Dataset for Input and Output

A collection of input datasets comes with the test suite (the StandardDataSets directory). Some input files are generated by the tests. The paths to the input are specified in the integration script. The output files are written to subdirectories in the TestProcedures directory.

Getting Started

In order to run the COLLADA conformance tests, your application must be able to

- Read and write COLLADA files

- Render a .PNG image at 512 x 512

- Include scriptable viewpoints and lights

The tests run on Windows machines only and take up a lot of memory.

Downloading and Installing the CTS

The CTS is available free of charge to anyone through the Khronos Implementer program available at www.khronos.org/conformance/implementers/collada/. Just create an account and download the package. The suite uses long file names that can cause problems on Windows systems by exceeding the 255-character (260 if you count D:\ and an invisible null at the end) path name limit. To avoid trouble, unzip the package in the root directory of your disk volume or some other directory with a short path name.

Prerequisites

The CTS requires only two prerequisites: the installation of some Python-related tools, and the Microsoft .NET Framework.

Python-related Tools

Before you can run the suite, you will need to install some Python-related tools, which you can find in the CTS\Prerequisites directory. These include Python itself, the Win32 extensions, wxPython and pyOpenGL. Even though the suite comes with the correct version of Python, you may have to install more than one version, but only if your application needs them; some do, some don't. Check the "add software" panel on your computer before installing anything to see if more recent versions of these tools are already installed. You must use the version numbers shown in this directory or higher. If your copy of Python isn't installed in the standard location, you may need to set its path in the config file. On Windows 7 and Vista, you have to install the Python tools as an administrator.

.NET Framework

Unless the Microsoft .NET Framework is installed, the framework won't be able to validate your COLLADA documents (MSXML is the default validator), and you won't be able to enable crash detection. You can disable crash detection or specify the timeout value in the config file.

Integration

Integration involves sending information back and forth between the test suite and the target application via a Python script, which you write, and a config file that you modify. The Python script generates and executes other scripts. To integrate your target application with the test suite, do the following:

- Create the Python script in the Scripts directory to map your application. You will usually copy and modify an existing script.

- Update config.txt in the top-level directory to set up your application path.

- Debug by running a small sample of the suite.

The Config File

The config file is held in the root of the CTS directory. Each line in the config file is a setting, with the description on the left and the value on the right. Update the config file with the path for your application. Be sure to use a tab delimiter between the key and value. (Watch for editors that convert tabs to spaces.) Do not leave a blank line at the end of the file.

The Python Script

The Scripts folder of the CTS directory holds a variety of integration scripts:

- FApplication is the basic script.

- FMax is the script for Autodesk 3ds Max.

- FMaya is the script for Autodesk Maya.

- FMimic is a bare bones script that includes a placeholder for a target application. It doesn't actually run an application, but it does let you run the tests.

- FXsi is the script for Autodesk Softimage.

To write or adapt a script, you should know the following:

- What the inputs are, where to find them, and what to do with them

- What outputs you produce and where they go

- The status codes you get and return

If your application doesn't support cameras and lighting and/or doesn't read camera and lighting parameters from the COLLADA document, you may have to set the camera and light positions in your Python script; you need cameras and lights in order to render and you must use the settings the tests require. You may need to delete your default lights and cameras so that the application properly renders the values in the COLLADA document.

Listing 6-1 shows some pseudo code, contributed by Simone Nicolò, a software engineer at Google, which shows how to write the log file for an import operation for SketchUp.

Listing 6-1. Pseudocode for Writing a Log File for a SketchUp Import Operation

```
Get the return value from Import
return_value = Sketchup.active_model.import "<model_path>"
then based on the return value write the log
if return_value
  # write 'Import Succeeded' to the log
else
  # write 'Import Failed' to the log
end
```

Your script will need to call the following methods in the following order:

- Init

- BeginScript

- WriteImport

- WriteRender

- WriteExport

- EndScript

- RunScript

- BeginScript

- WriteImport

- WriteRender

- EndScript

- RunScript

See the list of methods in HowToIntegrateSoftware.doc in the CTS\Documentation\HowtoAddSoftware directory, which also includes tips on dealing with cameras.

You will need to implement methods such as GetPrettyName(): return string, which passes information to the script that runs the target application. The script is run in the RunScript method. You can find all the methods in the complete COLLADA conformance test tutorial hosted by Khronos (see the "Useful Links" section).

The FApplication Script as a Model

The FApplication script in the `Scripts` directory provides useful information about methods, input, and output. Note the imported libraries:

- os (a Python module)

- os.path (a Python module)

- subprocess (a Python module)

- Core.Common.FUtils (resides in the `C:\CTS\Core\Common` directory). Gets and replaces filename extensions; determines whether a filename extension is that of an image file; determines whether a filename is a proper filename; gets directory names and paths; parses dates; and so on.

- Core.Common.FConstants (defines the constants the scripts use)

Class `FApplication` is the abstract class for the target application. The class defs can be found in the COLLADA CTS Tutorial.

Creating and Running the Tests

To start the test suite GUI, click the Python script COLLADATestSuite.py in the CTS root directory. Before you can run the tests for the first time, you must populate the test grid as follows:

- Create a new test procedure (File menu)

- Open the procedure you just created (File menu)

- Add tests (Test menu)

To run the tests with an existing procedure, just select File ➤ Open Test procedure, and the full test grid will appear.

Creating a Test Procedure

A test procedure comprises a series of tasks, some of which are repeated: import, export, render, and validate. Each task can generate one or more COLLADA documents and/or images. You must create and configure a test procedure before you can run any tests. Test procedures can be reused.

The input to a procedure is one or more data sets, which are found in the `StandardDataSets` subdirectory of the CTS hierarchy.

To create a new test procedure, select File ➤ New Test Procedure, and fill in the title: <Product Name> CTS Submission. For Trimble SketchUp, for example, your procedure name might be SketchUp_CTS_Submission. (Some test procedure names will not work with spaces.)

In the Add Operation box, select each of the tasks in the order specified here (which is not necessarily the order in which the operations appear in the box):

- Import ➤ *<ProductName>* ➤ Add. Import is the only task that requires a product name. The product name will appear in the right-hand window. (When you run the integration script, the name of your application will be added to the Import drop-down box.) See Figure 6-1.

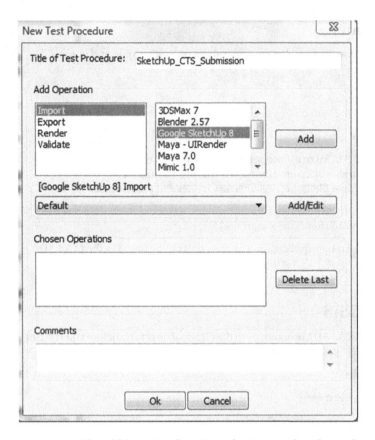

Figure 6-1. *The Add Operation box. First select Import, then the product name*

- Add Operation: Render ➤ Add. Note the Chosen Operations box. The operations must be selected and display in the proper order. Watch out: Export, which should be selected after Render, appears before Render in the Add Operation box.

- Add Operation: Export ➤ Add

- Add Operation: Import ➤ *<ProductName>* ➤ Add

- Add Operation: Render ➤ Add

- Add Operation: Validate ➤ MSXML 6.0 ➤ Add

You cannot add comments to a test procedure after it's been created, so do it now. You may add comments to test results at any time, however.

Select OK. You now have a test procedure and can add tests. You should also have a `TestProcedures` directory, which holds not only procedures, but also the output from the tests.

You can delete or rename a test procedure through Windows Explorer or the command-line window, or you can rename a procedure using the "Save Test Procedure As" icon in the toolbar above the column headings. You cannot delete a procedure through the test GUI, but you can delete a single test using the context menu in the GUI.

Adding Tests

Go to the Test menu and select Add Tests. The Test Settings dialog will come up. Configure any test settings your product needs. In most cases, Default will be sufficient. Press Next.

The tests expect an image size of 512 x 512, so be sure your images comply. Larger images could cause you to run out of memory. Smaller ones may not compare well enough to pass the test case. You can change the size in the Edit Settings dialog, which is reached by pressing Add/Edit on any of the operations shown in the Test Settings dialog. The Select Data Set dialog will come up. Select the following and press Finish:

- StandardDataSets/Collada
- StandardDataSets/xml

Confirm that there are 613 tests in the Total box on the toolbar. (The tests are numbered 0 through 612.) If not, you might not have selected all six operations or the two datasets you need. Try creating a new test procedure.

The Grid

Once the grid displays, you can use the menus, the toolbar, and the context commands on the right-click menu. Some context commands are available from every cell; some are cell-specific. See the list of the context menus in section 9.7 of the CTS manual, Context Menus. The CTS displays standard format images. If a format can't be displayed, you'll get a message to that effect.

Running the Tests

The input to the tests comes from the Standard Data Sets dialog box, which you can get to from the Tests ➤ Add Tests dialog.

Each test is composed of a COLLADA document (.dae file) and a judging script. Some of the scripts have different requirements for different badges, so it is possible to pass the Baseline level and not the Superior or Exemplary, or Baseline and Superior, but not Exemplary, for a given test. The description of the test is displayed in the Description column; it comes from the subject element in the .dae file.

For more information on what is being tested, see COLLADA_CTS_test_cases.xls in the CTS\TestCaseDocumentation directory. You can also check the judging scripts to see what each test is looking for. The judging scripts are contained in the StandardDataSets folder structure along with the COLLADA input document for each test.

Selecting Tests

You can launch all the tests or a portion of them from the Test menu. You can also run a single test from the context menu when the cursor is positioned in its row. Some tests depend on the successful completion of other tests, so don't (initially) run tests out of order.

You can select a range of tests by using the CTRL and/or SHIFT keys just as you do with any Windows application. Hold down the CTRL key while selecting more than one test. To select a block, highlight the topmost test, then hold SHIFT down while you select the last test in the sequence. All the tests in between the two will highlight and you can Run Selected from the Test menu.

There is no easy way to select only Baseline tests, but don't worry about that: there's no reason to do so. You have to run all the tests in order to earn a badge.

While the Tests Are Running

The CTS divides each test into three sections comprising one or more steps and runs them one after the other to minimize loading time for the target application. The steps, which correspond to the operations Import, Render, Export, and Validate in the order you set them up, are numbered 0 through 5; the test grid shows which number goes with which operation. In Figure 6-2, the scripts for steps 0, 1, and 2 have been created and executed; steps 3, 4, and 5 will run when the first batch has completed.

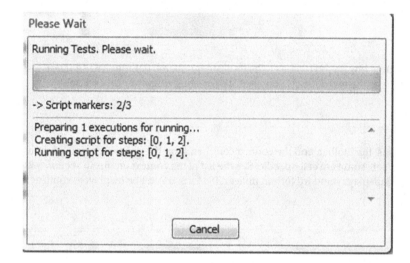

Figure 6-2. *The suite displays simple progress messages while the tests are running*

When a test crashes, the CTS attempts to locate the last test that completed and reruns the suite from there until it finds the test that crashed. Once you have fixed the issue that caused the test to crash, CTS will eventually manage to continue past the failing test. You can set crash detection to yes or no and specify the timeout value in the config file.

Canceling Tests

When you cancel the tests, the CTS waits until it reaches the next section before performing the cancel operation. Use the Task Manager to quit the CTS. Note that if you cancel, the suite ignores the entire run, and you have to start over. As a safeguard, you might want to run small groups of tests to begin with.

Reading the Results

When evaluating the results of a test, the most important columns to check are Results and the three badge columns. The Results column tells you whether the test worked as expected. Green means yes; red means that the test failed in some way. The three badge columns tell you whether the COLLADA files meet expectations. If they do, the column(s) will be green; if not, they will be red. It is possible for a Results column to be green and one or more badge columns to be red. This means that the test worked but a badge was not achieved because the target application failed to meet expectations, because it didn't handle the COLLADA documents properly, didn't render correctly, and so on.

When a test passes, you get messages that look like Figures 6-3 to 6-7.

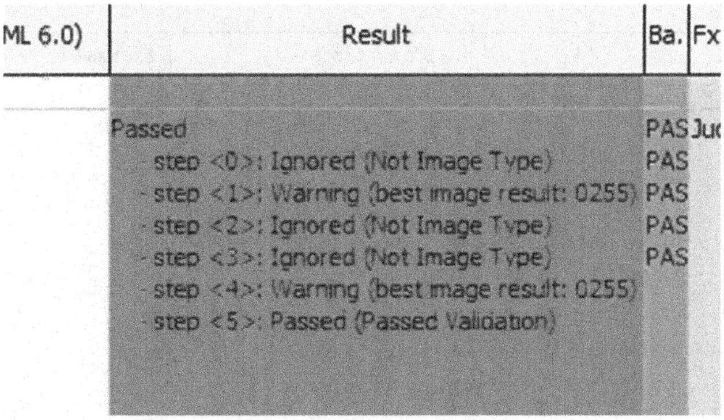

Figure 6-3. *A green (passed) indication in the Result column has nothing to do with badges. It simply means that the test executed properly (didn't crash)*

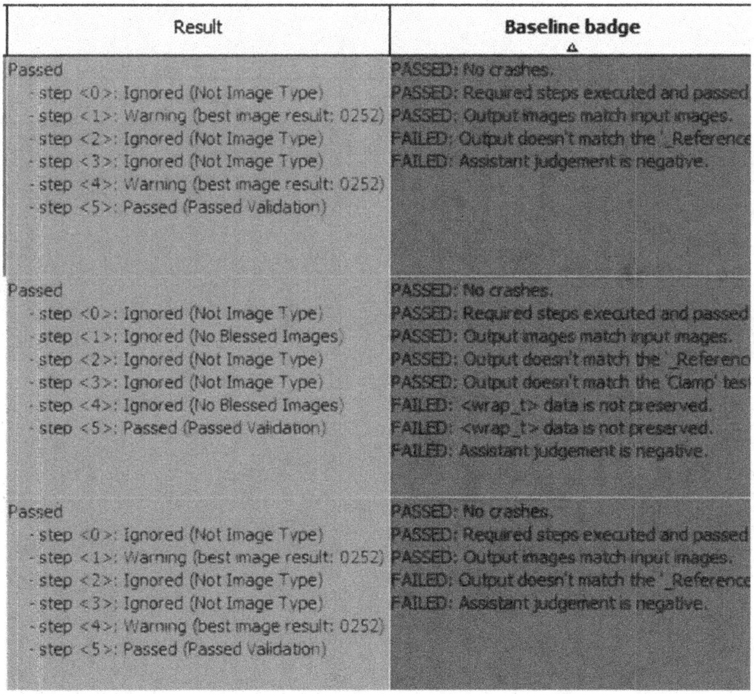

Figure 6-4. *Green in Result, red in badge: when the Result column is green, the test/application has run okay, but a badge wasn't awarded*

Total 613   Passed 111   Failed 5   No badges earned.

Result	Baseline badge	Superior badge	Exemplary badge
Passed - step <0>: Ignored (Not Image Type) - step <1>: Ignored (No Blessed Images) - step <2>: Ignored (Not Image Type) - step <3>: Ignored (Not Image Type) - step <4>: Ignored (No Blessed Images) - step <5>: Passed (Passed Validation)	PASSED: No crashes. PASSED: Required steps executed and passed.	FAILED: Number of animation images are too few. FAILED: Assistant judgement is negative.	Judgement failed.
Passed - step <0>: Ignored (Not Image Type) - step <1>: Ignored (No Blessed Images) - step <2>: Ignored (Not Image Type) - step <3>: Ignored (Not Image Type) - step <4>: Ignored (No Blessed Images) - step <5>: Passed (Passed Validation)	PASSED: No crashes. PASSED: Required steps executed and passed.	FAILED: Number of animation images are too few. FAILED: Assistant judgement is negative.	Judgement failed.

Figure 6-5. *Baseline only passed (only Result and Baseline columns are green)*

Failed 9   No badges earned.

Result	Baseline badge	Superior badge	Exemplary badge
Passed - step <0>: Ignored (Not Image Type) - step <1>: Ignored (No Blessed Images) - step <2>: Ignored (Not Image Type) - step <3>: Ignored (Not Image Type) - step <4>: Ignored (No Blessed Images) - step <5>: Passed (Passed Validation)	PASSED: No crashes. PASSED: Required steps executed and passed.	Judgement passed.	FAILED: Couldn't find keywords in output file. FAILED: <subject> data is not preserved. FAILED: <title> data is not preserved. FAILED: Assistant judgement is negative.
Passed - step <0>: Ignored (Not Image Type) - step <1>: Ignored (No Blessed Images) - step <2>: Ignored (Not Image Type) - step <3>: Ignored (Not Image Type) - step <4>: Ignored (No Blessed Images) - step <5>: Passed (Passed Validation)	PASSED: No crashes. PASSED: Required steps executed and passed. PASSED: <modified> element is correct.	Judgement passed.	Judgement passed.
Passed - step <0>: Ignored (Not Image Type) - step <1>: Ignored (No Blessed Images) - step <2>: Ignored (Not Image Type) - step <3>: Ignored (Not Image Type) - step <4>: Ignored (No Blessed Images) - step <5>: Passed (Passed Validation)	PASSED: No crashes. PASSED: Required steps executed and passed.	Judgement passed.	FAILED: <revision> data does not exist. FAILED: Assistant judgement is negative.

Figure 6-6. *Baseline and Superior passed, but some of the tests failed the Exemplary level*

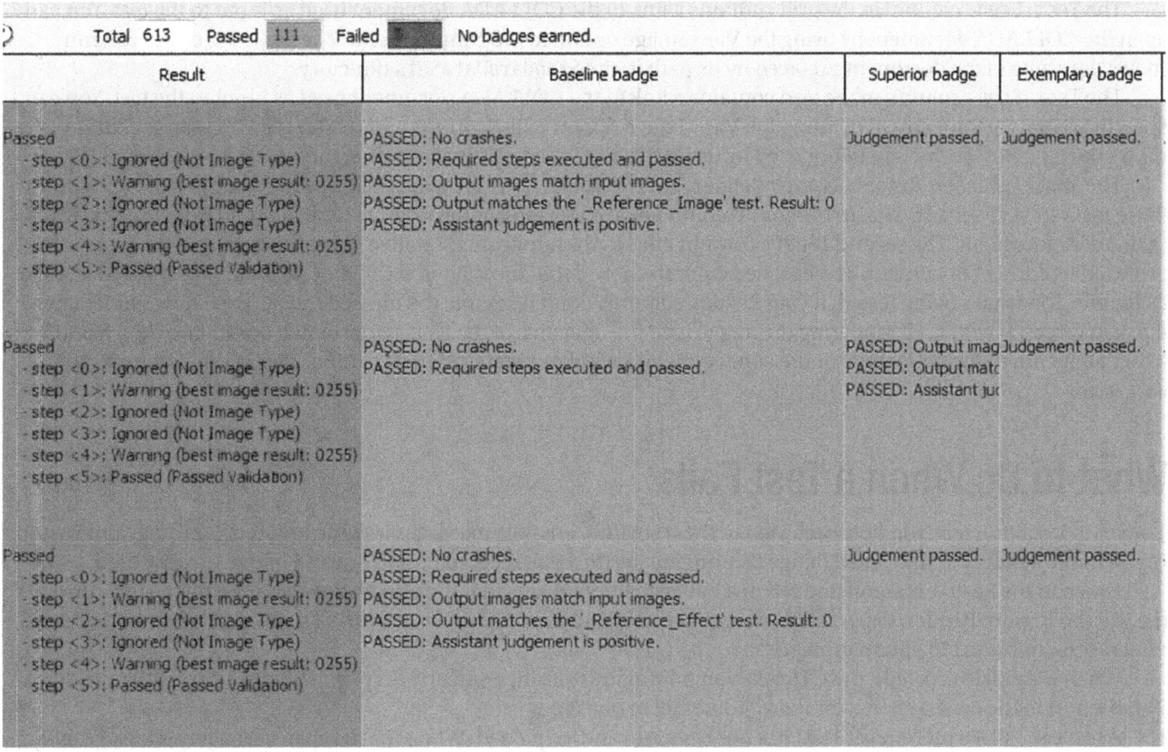

Total 613   Passed 111   Failed   No badges earned.

Result	Baseline badge	Superior badge	Exemplary badge
Passed - step <0>: Ignored (Not Image Type) - step <1>: Warning (best image result: 0255) - step <2>: Ignored (Not Image Type) - step <3>: Ignored (Not Image Type) - step <4>: Warning (best image result: 0255) - step <5>: Passed (Passed Validation)	PASSED: No crashes. PASSED: Required steps executed and passed. PASSED: Output images match input images. PASSED: Output matches the '_Reference_Image' test. Result: 0 PASSED: Assistant judgement is positive.	Judgement passed.	Judgement passed.
Passed - step <0>: Ignored (Not Image Type) - step <1>: Warning (best image result: 0255) - step <2>: Ignored (Not Image Type) - step <3>: Ignored (Not Image Type) - step <4>: Warning (best image result: 0255) - step <5>: Passed (Passed Validation)	PASSED: No crashes. PASSED: Required steps executed and passed.	PASSED: Output imag PASSED: Output matc PASSED: Assistant ju	Judgement passed.
Passed - step <0>: Ignored (Not Image Type) - step <1>: Warning (best image result: 0255) - step <2>: Ignored (Not Image Type) - step <3>: Ignored (Not Image Type) - step <4>: Warning (best image result: 0255) step <5>: Passed (Passed Validation)	PASSED: No crashes. PASSED: Required steps executed and passed. PASSED: Output images match input images. PASSED: Output matches the '_Reference_Effect' test. Result: 0 PASSED: Assistant judgement is positive.	Judgement passed.	Judgement passed.

Figure 6-7. *Test run successfully and all levels passed*

You can add comments to a test's row by double-clicking in the Comments cell, as shown in Figure 6-8.

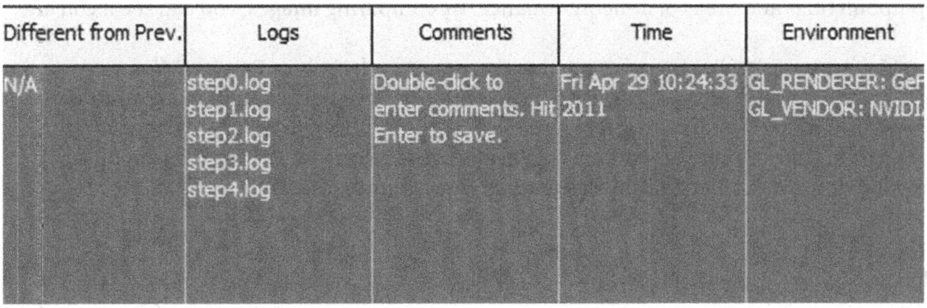

Different from Prev.	Logs	Comments	Time	Environment
N/A	step0.log step1.log step2.log step3.log step4.log	Double-click to enter comments. Hit Enter to save.	Fri Apr 29 10:24:33 2011	GL_RENDERER: GeF GL_VENDOR: NVIDI

Figure 6-8. *The Comments cell*

The Test Scene column in the grid contains a link to the COLLADA document used as input to the test. You can open the COLLADA document by using the View Image option in the context menu. The Test Filename column shows the name of the document prefaced by its path in the StandardDataSets directory.

The Test Scene column in the grid contains a link to the COLLADA document used as input to the test. You can open the COLLADA document by using the View Image option in the context menu. The Test Filename column shows the name of the document prefaced by its path in the StandardDataSets directory.

The Import, Render, Export, Import, Render, and Validate columns contain links to the output from each of those tasks for a given test. The first Import column links to the application's native file generated from the Test Scene COLLADA document. The second Import column links to the application's native file generated from the first cycle's exported COLLADA document. The Blessed column shows what the rendered COLLADA document should look like. Depending on what's being tested, if your Render columns don't resemble the blessed image, you know immediately that something is wrong. (If rendering the image isn't the objective of the test, a non-match doesn't matter.) Don't worry about anything the manual or the context menu says about blessing an execution. This is a legacy item that isn't used.

What to Do When a Test Fails

The Result column tells you how each step in the test fared. Possible messages include Ignored, Warning, and Passed. Green in the Result column and a badge column means the test executed correctly and a badge was awarded.

Green in the Result column and red in a badge column means that the application can execute the test correctly (i.e., all the Import/Render/Export steps were successful) but the output files are not COLLADA conformant. When a test crashes, the Result column turns red.

When a Validate task fails, the CTS tells you how many warnings and errors you got. View the errors by clicking on View Report in the context menu for the Validate cell in question.

A test can fail if a prerequisite test has not been run and/or passed. When that happens, you get a message telling you which test(s) you need to run, by name, not test number (e.g., "_Reference _Oneimage test case"). However, if you run the suite in the order presented, you shouldn't encounter this situation.

Comparing Test Runs

Comparing test runs helps pinpoint bugs and areas of nonconformance. By comparing images, you can see if you are getting warmer or colder.

To see the results of a previous test, right-click anywhere in the test row and select Show Previous. You can tell which tests have been run more than once by checking the Different from Previous column. You can delete an execution from the GUI by right-clicking the test and selecting Delete Execution. The histories are stored in the TestProcedures directory. When you compare executions, the results of the selected tests display in a pop-up window. Beware, though: executions are described only by date and sequence number, so keep track!

Comparing Images

Comparing images helps you diagnose problems in your application. You can compare your results with Khronos's blessed images or with images you've produced during different test runs or steps (see Figure 6-9). Comparing images involves three dialog boxes: "Compare Image With," where you select the images you want to use; "Image Comparison," where you actually look at the images side by side; and "Image Diff," which shows you the pixel-by-pixel differences.

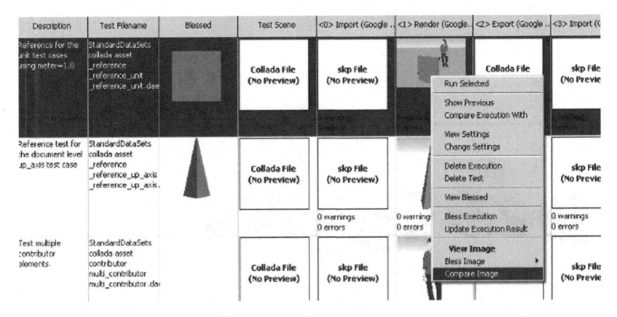

Figure 6-9. *Use the context menu on the image you want to compare*

The "Compare Image With" Dialog

To compare images generated by a particular test with blessed images or with other images your application has produced during conformance testing, select the thumbnail for the image in question and bring up the context menu. Select Compare Image. You can include the blessed image in your comparison, but you cannot choose only the blessed image; you must also select another image generated during testing, either as output from a different step, or from a different execution, or from a different test, or from a different test procedure. Fortunately, you don't have to remember every place you've generated a like image; the drop-down menu in the dialog shows you the options, and you select from those. Steps are numbered 0-5; different executions are identified by date and sequence number. If there are no valid different tests or test procedures, those choices will be disabled.

The "Image Comparison" Dialog

In this box, the images you've selected are displayed side by side. If you've included the blessed image, you'll see it on the far left. The reference image—the one from the test you highlighted in the GUI—displays in the middle, and the image you've chosen to compare with is on the right. Metadata about the test and the execution date and sequence appears above. If your image is part of an animation, you can page through the frames with the arrows.

In Figure 6-10, you can see that there's a shader problem in the tested image: the link on the left has no shading at all.

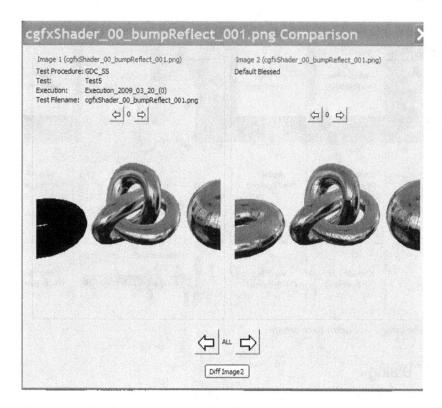

Figure 6-10. *The "Image Comparison" dialog*

The "Image Diff" Dialog

The "Image Diff" box shows you the absolute and relative differences between your image and either the blessed or the comparison image (see Figure 6-11). The absolute pixel-by-pixel difference displays on the left side of the Image Diff box. On the right is the grayscale relative difference where the most different pixels are shown in white. To compare your image with the blessed image, press Different Blessed. To compare your image with the comparison image, press Diff Image2. You can only make one comparison at a time.

CHAPTER 6 ▓ BUILDING A ROCK-SOLID CONTENT PIPELINE WITH THE COLLADA CONFORMANCE TEST SUITE

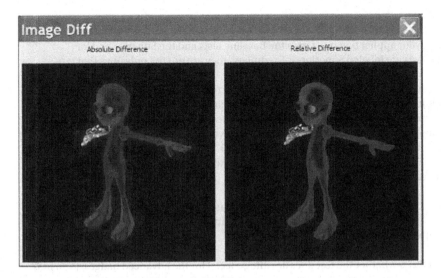

Figure 6-11. Another image comparison

Because the absolute difference is calculated by subtracting one set of pixels from the other, the result shows you where there are rendering deviations. (If the images are exactly the same, the absolute difference will come out black, so the blacker the absolute difference, the more the images match.) The relative difference is the grayscale representation of those absolute differences normalized. The magnitude of the greatest difference is shown as white, which means that anywhere you see white, the relative difference image differs most from the comparison image.

Troubleshooting

You will find troubleshooting help for specific tests and conditions within the GUI test reports. However, here are some general tips.

Setup

If the test suite will not launch, run the Python script from the command line to see error reports. If wx or OpenGL is mentioned, make sure you installed both packages into the correct Python version. If your script code doesn't compile, the suite will not launch. Rendering .PNG images at a resolution greater than 512 x 512 could cause memory problems. If your output document is significantly larger than your input document, you will get a warning. You won't fail the test, but do follow these recommendations to avoid excessive growth of documents:

- Strip non-significant leading/trailing zeros from numbers in the output.

- Keep XML output indentations to a reasonable minimum. Two spaces or one hard tab per level is sufficient.

- Avoid indentations when writing large arrays or lists of numbers. Write them as a single long line of text with separating spaces or break them into multiple non-indented lines.

Judging Scripts

To achieve a badge beyond Baseline, your application must pass the Baseline tests and the Superior and/or Exemplary tests. Even though some tests are labeled Superior or Exemplary, they are not the only ones that test advanced capabilities.

Each test comes with a judging script that looks at the outputs and status returns from the test. The judging scripts are stored with the test cases in the StandardDataSets directory. You have to drill down to the lowest level of a directory to find them; they're stored at the same level as the .dae file input to the test. These files contain useful information about what the test is looking for in order to satisfy each badge level.

For example, if you look at the multi_contributor judging script (Test ID 0711, #2 on the grid) in the folder C:\CTS\StandardDataSets\collada\library_geometries\geometry\asset\contributor\, you will see that this test involves all three badge levels and deals with them like this:

```
# JudgeBaseline: just verifies that the standard steps did not crash.
# JudgeSuperior: also verifies that the validation steps are not in error.
# JudgeExemplary: same as intermediate badge.
```

These comments will quickly tell you whether the test does anything special for the advanced badges. (You may also want to check the code to make sure they're correct. There are cases in which the comments contradict the code.) In this case, the Superior level and Exemplary levels require that the target application meet additional criteria.

You see also that at the Baseline level, not only must the test not crash, but import/export/validate must exist and pass, while render must only exist.

You can verify which operations the test is performing in the code. Only import, export, and validate are used. Render is absent.

```
self.__assistant.CheckSteps(context, ["Import", "Export", "Validate"], [])
```

However, in a script like C:\CTS\StandardDataSets\collada\library_cameras\camera_reference_reference_optics_orthographic_zfar_z_near (Test ID 0106, #90 on the grid), all the operations are necessary.

```
self.__assistant.CheckSteps(context, ["Import", "Export", "Validate"], ["Render"])
```

The Render operation must exist because at the Superior level, the rendered images are compared, in this line:

```
self.__assistant.CompareRenderedImages(context)
```

The multi_contributor script tests all the levels separately, returning unique results for each, but the camera script tests only the Baseline and Superior levels, returning the same result for both the Superior and Exemplary levels.

The Judging Script Driver

The judging script for each test passes parameters to the judging driver script, FResult, which is stored in the C:\CTS\Core\Logic directory. The judging script status codes govern what goes in the badge and results columns in the GUI; see Listing 6-2.

Listing 6-2. Judging Script Status Codes and Their Meanings

```
PASSED_IMAGE = 0
    PASSED_ANIMATION = 1
    PASSED_VALIDATION = 2
    FAILED_IMAGE = 3
    FAILED_ANIMATION = 4
```

```
FAILED_VALIDATION = 5
FAILED_MISSING = 6
IGNORED_TYPE = 7
IGNORED_NO_BLESS_IMAGE = 8
IGNORED_NO_BLESS_ANIMATION = 9
IGNORED_NONE = 10
CRASH = 11
```

The COLLADA Input Documents

You can look at the COLLADA input documents to see what you're trying to process. For example, using the tests from the judging script section, look at the accompanying .dae input files, C:\CTS\StandardDataSets\collada\library_geometries\geometry\asset\contributor\multi_contributor.DAE and C:\CTS\StandardDataSets\collada\library_cameras\camera_reference_reference_optics_orthographic_zfar_z_near_reference_optics_orthographic_zfar_z_near.DAE.

The multi-contributor document contains two contributors (one of whom is Bugs Bunny). The camera document contains a main camera with the attributes shown in Listing 6-3.

Listing 6-3. Main Camera Attributes in the CTS Input

```
<library_cameras>
        <camera id="mainCamera" name="mainCamera">
            <optics>
                <technique_common>
                    <orthographic>
                        <ymag>100</ymag>
                        <aspect_ratio>1</aspect_ratio>
                        <znear>0.1</znear>
                        <zfar>5000</zfar>
                    </orthographic>
                </technique_common>
            </optics>
        </camera>
    </library_cameras>
```

All the COLLADA input files are available in the StandardDataSets directory. You can open them directly from the GUI by selecting the Test Scene cell, then View Image from the context menu.

The COLLADA Output Documents

You can see what you're generating by examining your COLLADA output documents. There are two ways to view them:

- Right-click the export column and select View Image, then Text Only. Even though the menu item says View Image, you get a text file.

- Look in the Test Procedures directory. Drill down from the test number through the specific execution to the desired step.

Documentation

In the CTS Documentation directory, you will find

- The CTS Manual (CTSManual.doc)

- A COLLADA CTF How To (CTF_How_To.doc) that covers setup, fixing Autodesk Maya® errors, creating and running a simple test procedure, how to create your own test, and how to add a test to a local copy of the framework.

- A brief overview (README.doc) that explains how to create a test procedure and submit results.

- In the subdirectory HowToAddSoftware, see the HowToIntegrateSoftware.doc, which describes the methods you'll need in your integration script.

There are two Python scripts in the Scripts subdirectory of HowToAddSoftware: FDebug and FMimic. FDebug helps you debug your integration script by printing a message and parameters for all steps. FMimic is a simple renderer that attempts to pass by copying the input and providing a single test image. It is used to validate that this type of renderer cannot pass the conformance suite. It also serves as a good example for command-line tools that want to integrate with the suite.

References

The Khronos Group hosts the complete COLLADA CTS Tutorial at www.khronos.org/files/collada/COLLADA-CTS-Tutorial.pdf.

The test suite code is available at https://github.com/KhronosGroup/COLLADA-CTS.

The Khronos Group hosts the official COLLADA web page at http://khronos.org/collada.

A public COLLADA mailing list at www.khronos.org/collada/public-mailing-list/ has been created specifically for asking questions and reporting bugs about the conformance tests.

There is a Twitter group at http://twitter.com/collada and a Facebook page at www.facebook.com/people/Collada-Duck/100000363377190.

The authors can be contacted at remi@acm.org and paula@writingshow.com.

CHAPTER 7

■ ■ ■

Rendering COLLADA Assets on Mac OS X with Scene Kit

Fabrice Robinet

Since Snow Leopard (10.6) was released in 2009, OS X has provided built-in support for COLLADA assets. So far, this support has enabled visualization of COLLADA assets in Preview and Quick Look. Developers using Quartz Composer have also been able to render COLLADA assets in their compositions, but until now, an API was still to be exposed. Now, with Mountain Lion (10.8), OS X has introduced a new 3D framework called Scene Kit that adds significant COLLADA functionality.

This chapter explains how to use Scene Kit to render COLLADA assets. Incorporating a worked example, it offers an overview of Scene Kit and its relationship to COLLADA; shows how to integrate Scene Kit with Xcode; presents key aspects of the Scene Kit API[1] like COLLADA scene import and scene graph manipulations, animations, and rendering; and touches on more advanced topics such as custom rendering.

To get the most out of this chapter, it is recommended but not required that you have a basic knowledge of COLLADA and a working knowledge of Objective-C.[2]

Integrating Scene Kit with Xcode

Scene Kit provides its own view in the Xcode Object Library. By selecting a Scene View and adding it to the project as shown in Figure 7-1, you instantiate a new SCNView.

---

[1]Apple Inc. "Scene Kit Framework Reference." http://developer.apple.com/library/mac/#documentation/SceneKit/Reference/SceneKit_Framework/index.html.
[2]Apple Inc. "The Objective-C Programming Language." http://developer.apple.com/library/mac/#documentation/Cocoa/Conceptual/ObjectiveC/Introduction/introObjectiveC.html.

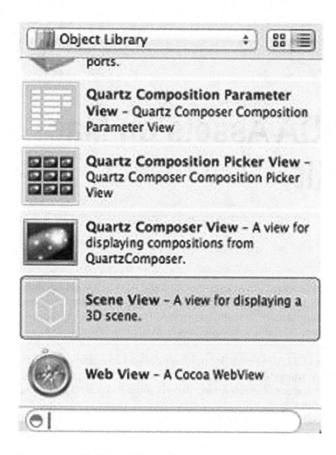

Figure 7-1. *The Xcode Object Library*

SCNView has its own inspector that exposes the following capabilities:

- **Scene:** The developer can assign a COLLADA file (.dae) from the project resources.

- **Background:** Sets the background color of the SCNView.

- **Behavior:** Allows mouse and touch events to control the camera.

- **Jittering:** Triggers a much-refined anti-aliased result by accumulating many renderings of still frames (occurs only when the scene has no animation running and the user is not interacting with the view).

- **Multisampling:** Features wrapper-to-OpenGL multisampling.

- **Enable default lighting:** Provides omni light that enlightens the scene.

The Xcode COLLADA Editor

Xcode 4.4 has been enhanced with new editing functionalities for COLLADA assets, including new inspectors for nodes, materials, lights and a tree view to inspect node hierarchy. The scope of the editing functionalities matches the possibilities exposed by the Scene Kit API. The edited scene can be re-exported to replace the current document. Doing so allows the scene to be adjusted precisely for the Scene Kit runtime.

As shown in Figure 7-2, the left part of the editor contains a tree view of the scene graph; in the middle part, the scene is rendered and updated live when you change parameters in the inspector on the right side.

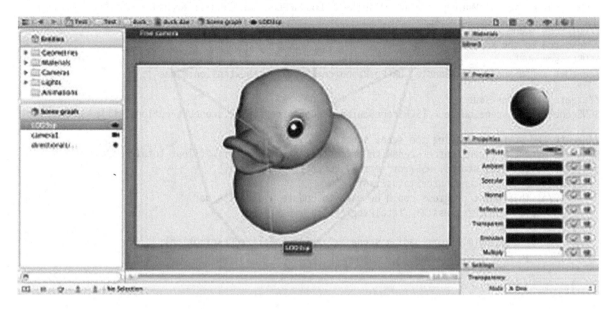

Figure 7-2. *Scene view editor*

It is worth mentioning that this editing should be used only to "finalize" a scene. The original file from the authoring tool should always be preserved in order to regenerate the original COLLADA file if needed.

The Scene Kit API

The following sections present an overview of how to use the Scene Kit API.

COLLADA Scene Import

The Scene Kit API supports COLLADA assets exclusively, but the API isn't strictly tied to COLLADA and looks generic enough to support other kinds of assets in the future. This section covers the usage of the SCNSceneSource class, which implements the following features:

- Loading a COLLADA scene
- Extraction of COLLADA library entries

As an aside, readers familiar with OS X SDK will find the API to load COLLADA scenes similar to the ImageIO API to load images.

Loading a COLLADA Scene

The most straightforward way to import a COLLADA scene is to use the following method, which returns a new SCNScene instance:

```
+ (SCNScene *)sceneWithURL:(NSURL *)url options:(NSDictionary *)options error:(NSError **)error;
```

Using SCNSceneSource is required to access more information such as progress updates.

Listing 7-1 shows how to use sceneWithOptions:statusHandler: to load a scene and get updates inside a block.

Listing 7-1. Using sceneWithOptions:statusHandler: to Load a Scene and Get Updates Inside a Block

```
//our test scene is the famous COLLADA duck that we added as a
//resource to the Xcode project
NSURL* sceneURL;
sceneURL = [[NSBundle mainBundle] URLForResource:@"duck" withExtension:@"dae"];

//create the scene source
SCNSceneSource* sceneSource = [SCNSceneSource sceneSourceWithURL:sceneURL options:nil];

//create the scene by loading the scene source
SCNScene* scene = [sceneSource sceneWithOptions:nil statusHandler: ^(float totalProgress,
SCNSceneSourceStatus status, NSError* error, BOOL* stopLoading) {
    if (status != SCNSceneSourceStatusError) {
        //at this point progress could be used to update a progress bar
        NSLog(@" totalProgress:%f",totalProgress);
            } else {
                NSLog(@"Error loading scene %@",error.localizedDescription);
            }
        }
];
```

So far, the method sceneWithOptions: was called with nil for options. But the options available at loading time can be very useful. An efficient COLLADA viewer can easily be built up by passing the following set of options to the scene source:

- SCNSceneSourceCreateNormalsIfAbsentKey automatically computes normals for a given model.

- SCNSceneSourceFlattenSceneKey merges together all the geometries contained in the scene graph. When the asset has animations related to nodes containing geometry, the merge is not performed and the scene is left unchanged.

Listing 7-2 shows how to build the dictionary to be passed to the sceneWithOptions: method.

Listing 7-2. Building the Dictionary to be Passed to the sceneWithOptions: Method

```
NSDictionary *options;
options = [NSDictionary dictionaryWithObjectsAndKeys:
SCNSceneSourceFlattenSceneKey, @YES, SCNSceneSourceCreateNormalsIfAbsentKey,@YES, nil];
```

Additional details to complete a simple viewer setup are provided in the rendering section.

Extraction of COLLADA Library Entries

Beyond its typical usage in a viewer, a COLLADA asset can be considered a library of 3D entities (geometries, lights, etc.) to be organized at runtime by the application. Therefore, the SCNSceneSource class provides methods to extract these entities by simply referring to their unique COLLADA ID.

The first method retrieves all the identifiers for the entries of a given class.

```
- (NSArray *)identifiersOfEntriesWithClass:(Class)entryClass;
```

The second method simply returns the entry given its identifier.

```
-(id)entryWithIdentifier:(NSString*)id withClass:(Class)entryClass;
```

It is important to note that the entries in the libraries not referenced by the scene graph can be retrieved only using SCNSceneSource. These entries can be added to the scene graph programmatically.

Scene Graph Manipulation and Animations

Now you'll create an example to get familiar with the Scene Kit API and its scene graph. Through the creation of a simple "asteroid field," this example will demonstrate the following API features:

- Node retrieval, cloning, and addition in the scene graph

- Creation and manipulation of transforms, lights, and cameras

- Both explicit and implicit animation of node properties

To illustrate these features, let's split the example into three phases:

- Scene configuration

- Asteroid field instantiation and layout

- Asteroid field animation

Scene Configuration

This section shows how to build the asteroid scene from scratch. The asteroid is imported from a scene that contains it alone. This is an ideal setup to illustrate our point. You can use the API to create one instance of the camera and duplicate the asteroid node many times to produce an interesting display. Also, you can add an omnidirectional (omni) light and render the mesh using a bump-mapped material to improve the realism of the rendering.

Let's start creating the scene.

```
SCNScene* scene = [SCNScene scene];
```

Now you'll create the camera, which by default comes as a perspective camera. You'll also set up the zNear and zFar values for the viewing frustum.

```
SCNCamera* camera = [SCNCamera camera];
camera.zNear = 0.01;
camera.zFar = 100.0;
```

Once this camera is created, it still needs to be added to the scene graph. To do so, you need to create a node to hold it. Here is how to achieve this:

```
SCNNode* viewPoint = [SCNNode node];
viewPoint.camera = camera;
```

And finally, you add this node to the scene graph simply by adding it to the scene's root node.

```
[scene.rootNode addChildNode:viewPoint];
```

A similar pattern applies to creating the omni light.

```
SCNLight* light = [SCNLight light];
light.type = SCNLightTypeOmni;
SCNNode* lightNode = [SCNNode node];
lightNode.light = light;
[scene.rootNode addChildNode:lightNode];
```

Asteroid Field Instantiation and Layout

Now you'll instantiate and lay out the asteroid field. First, let's retrieve the asteroid node to be cloned.

```
SCNNode *referenceNode =  [referenceScene.rootNode childNodeWithName:@"asteroid" recursively:YES];
```

The node is cloned many times.

```
SCNNode* aClone = [referenceNode clone];
```

The method signatures above should be self-explanatory. However, one thing to note is that the clone—as expected—does not perform a deep copy of the node attributes; it just retains them. Practically, this means that meshes for cloned nodes will be shared, allowing better memory usage and performance, and that's especially important for this example.

Then, it's just a matter of duplicating the node at different positions. In the following code, FRAND returns a random number between 0 and MAX:

```
for (i= 0 ; i < MAX_NODES ; i++) {
      SCNNode* aClone = [referenceNode clone];
      aClone.position = SCNVector3Make(FRAND(MAX) - MAX/2.., FRAND(MAX) - MAX/2., -zDistance);
      [rootNode addChildNode:aClone];
}
```

Asteroid Field Animation

To set up the animation of the cloned nodes, you will change the instantiation scheme of the asteroid fields a bit. You will build an animation that creates one node at a time; each node will have its own animation and its "life" will be tied to its animation. You create a method called setupAsteroidAnimationForNode that takes the clone created as shown above. Within this method you build up an animation whose duration is four seconds.

Scene Kit is fully compatible with Core Animation and relies on its CAAnimation class to add animations to a node. The reader is encouraged to read the Core Animation programming guide.[3]

Even though not strictly needed by CAAnimation, you invoke setValue:forKey: on the animation object. This allows you to retrieve the node later on when the delegate that indicates the end of the animation has its method animationDidStop called. Listing 7-3 shows how to perform these tasks.

---

[3]Apple Inc. "Core Animation Programming Guide." http://developer.apple.com/library/ios/#DOCUMENTATION/Cocoa/ Conceptual/CoreAnimation_guide/Introduction/Introduction.html.

Listing 7-3. Setting up the Animation of the Cloned Nodes

```
- (void) setupAsteroidAnimationForNode:(SCNNode*)aClone
{
    CABasicAnimation *positionAnimation;
    SCNVector3 position = aClone.position;
    positionAnimation=[CABasicAnimation animationWithKeyPath:@"position"];
    positionAnimation.duration=4.0;
    positionAnimation.repeatCount=0;
    position.z = 0;
    positionAnimation.toValue= [NSValue valueWithSCNVector3:position];
    [positionAnimation setValue:aClone forKey:@"node"]; //we keep track of the node.
    positionAnimation.delegate = self;
    [aClone addAnimation:positionAnimation forKey:@"position"];
```

When the animation is over, the method `animationDidStop` is called within the delegate, and the node is removed by calling `removeFromParentNode`. As stated above, you can retrieve the node from the animation because it was explicitly added in `setupAsteroidAnimationForNode`. See Figure 7-3 for the code in action.

```
-(void)animationDidStop:(CAAnimation *)anim finished:(BOOL)flag {
    SCNNode* node = [anim valueForKey:@"node"];

    [node removeFromParentNode];
}
```

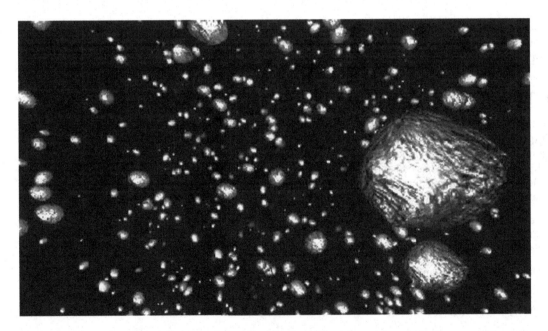

Figure 7-3. *Screenshot from the asteroid sample code. Asteroid mesh courtesy of fl4re Inc.* www.fl4re.com

Rendering

Scene Kit offers ways to customize rendering at many levels. However, because rendering deserves a whole chapter of its own, this section will give just a brief overview.

At the lowest level, an SCNRenderer instance handles the core rendering of the layers and views. It is possible to instantiate an SCNRenderer and pass an OpenGLContext context. Doing so provides more control over the rendering. For example, you might want to realize advanced post-processing effects not by drawing directly to the OpenGL framebuffer, but by drawing in a texture and processing that texture afterwards (using OpenGL Frame Buffer Objects).

But just for simple tweaks like customizing the background or drawing an overlay, there is an easier approach that involves taking advantage of the SCNSceneRendererDelegate protocol: both SCNView and SCNLayer implement this protocol. The delegate on the client side can implement the following methods:

- (void)renderer:(id <SCNSceneRenderer>)aRenderer willRenderScene:(SCNScene *) scene atTime:(NSTimeInterval)time;

- (void)renderer:(id <SCNSceneRenderer>)aRenderer didRenderScene:(SCNScene *) scene atTime:(NSTimeInterval)time;

Typically, willRenderScene:atTime: is suitable to draw a custom background and didRenderScene:atTime: is a good fit for an overlay.

Both SCNRenderer and SCNRendererDelegate operate at the scene level.

It is possible to replace and/or customize the rendering at the node level, such as for each SCNNode.

SCNNode owns a property called rendererDelegate, which expects to be assigned an SCNNodeRendererDelegate. Once that is done, Scene Kit will no longer perform any rendering for this particular node, but will call the delegate with the following method:

```
- (void)renderNode:(SCNNode *)node renderer:(SCNRenderer *)renderer arguments:(NSDictionary *)
arguments;
```

Even though no rendering is done, the scene graph is still evaluated, including the running animation. This means that the delegate can access matrices being animated, take advantage of the whole scene graph structure, and still be able to override the Scene Kit rendering with its own.

Relationship to COLLADA

It is well known that COLLADA is a dense specification allowing a lot of flexibility that makes supporting it exhaustively quite challenging. It is also common knowledge that Apple delivers a simple but powerful set of consistent graphic APIs for OS X developers (ImageKit, Core Image, Core Animation, etc.). Because Scene Kit is a high-level Objective-C API, Apple has had to make choices regarding the set of supported and exposed COLLADA features. While both COLLADA and Scene Kit provide a scene graph and common 3D entities such as nodes, cameras, lights, and materials, there are many differences, including the following:

- Scene Kit does not implement a stack of transforms; only one transform per node is supported. The consequence is that animations with transformed nodes are typically flattened before being imported into Scene Kit in order to satisfy this constraint.

- Only one light, mesh, and camera are allowed per node. This limitation leads to a simpler API.

- Scene Kit has added new properties to leverage features of its renderer, such as litPerPixel to specify whether lighting is performed at the pixel or at the vertex level.

Conclusion

This chapter provided information to get you started efficiently with Scene Kit. The reader is encouraged to explore more advanced features such as parametric geometry (cubes, capsules, torus, 3D text, and more), custom shaders, and access to imported geometry information (vertices and indices).

CHAPTER 8

■ ■ ■

COLLADA Exporter for Unity Developers in the Unity Asset Store

Rita Turkowski and Rémi Arnaud

Many Unity customers want to be able to export their work into other applications in the COLLADA format. We offer an exporter to do just that, and it is now available at the Unity Asset Store (see Figure 8-1). This chapter explains how to use the utility.

Figure 8-1. *The COLLADA Exporter inside the Unity Asset Store*

Introduction

With this extension to the Unity editor's File menu, you can take your finished work from Unity to any COLLADA (.dae format) importing application, such as Apple's Preview or iBook, Photoshop, Autodesk 3ds Max or Maya, Google Earth, SketchUp, (even back into Unity!), as well as most digital content creation tools—even your own applications.

Understanding the COLLADA Exporter for Unity

The extension is very easy to set up and use. To set up/install, simply take the downloaded .dll file (and optional collada_exporter.XmlSerializers if desired) and move it/them into the Editor drop-down under the Unity Project window, as shown in Figure 8-2.

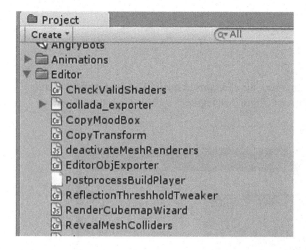

Figure 8-2. *The Unity editor Project window with the COLLADA Exporter installed*

The COLLADA exporter should appear on the File menu. If not, simply drag the downloaded .dll file and drop it into the Editor section under the Unity Project window, as shown in Figure 8-3.

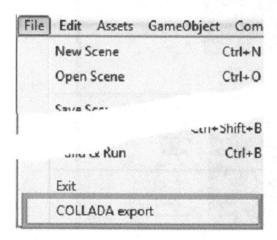

Figure 8-3. *The COLLADA export option in the Unity editor File menu*

Clicking the menu entry will give you the COLLADA Exporter dialog box, as shown in Figure 8-4. This is where you will specify all your parameters.

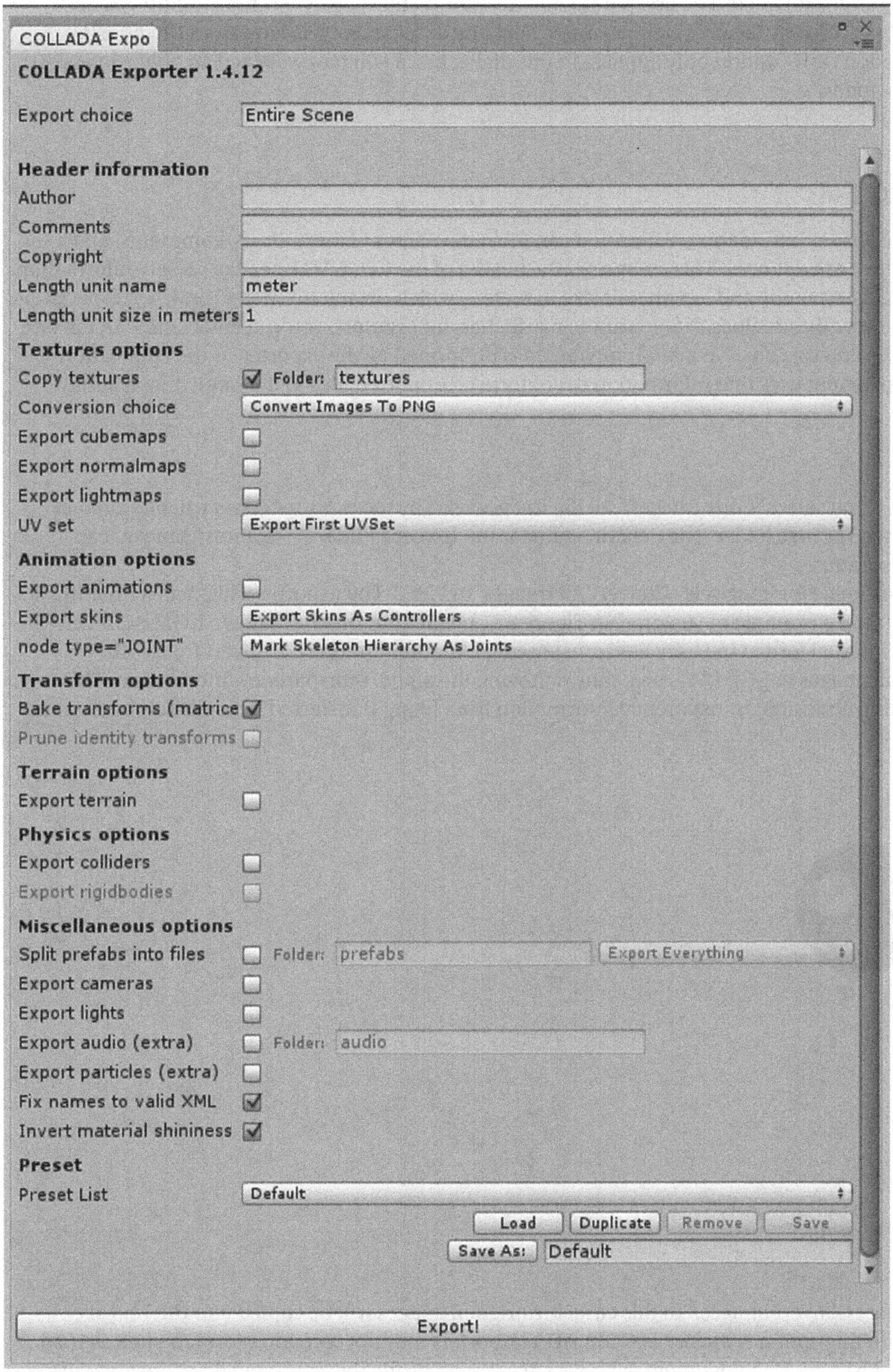

Figure 8-4. *The COLLADA Exporter dialog*

The COLLADA Exporter in Depth

From the top, here is the exporter explained. The first parameter, the export choice, may be either "Entire Scene" (the default when nothing is selected by the user), or you may select one or several objects to export by choosing "Selection Only." The "Selection Only" option only appears in this dialog box if you have selected an object to export from your scene or project window.

Header Information

The first set of options is the header information, where you can fill in the names of the authors, comments, and copyright information; all these are optional. This comprises the header of the COLLADA header <asset> information.

Then you have the length unit name and length unit size in meters, which default to "meter" and "1," respectively. To change the unit, just type over these values. If you want to use inches, for example, you can enter "inch" in the unit name box and "0.0254" in the unit size box. No actual conversion is performed by the exporter, as the application importing the COLLADA document uses that information to conform all imported files to the same dimensions.

Texture Options

In the copy textures option, if you select "Copy Images," all the images used by the exported Asset will be stored in subdirectories provided in the Texture folder. The default name for the Texture folder is "textures," but you can change that to whatever you want.

The default conversion choice for images is "Convert All Images To PNG." The exporter will create either RGB (24) or RGBA (32) textures (see an example of "texture" in Figure 8-5, taken from the well-known COLLADA Duck) depending on whether the internal format in Unity has transparency. Another option is "Convert Images To PNG 24;" this will convert all images to RGB (24) .png, thus removing the alpha/transparency information. This option is useful for preventing undesired transparency information from being transferred when the alpha channel is not used for transparency.

Figure 8-5. *COLLADA Duck "texture"*

The last option is "Do Not Convert Images." In this case, the original images will be copied into the Texture folder directly. The issue with this option is that most COLLADA importers may not recognize formats such as .psd. Whichever choice is made, the COLLADA document will reference the image file that was copied or converted. If "Texture copy" is set to "Do Not Copy Images," the images won't be copied, but the conversion choice parameter will still be used as references in the COLLADA document. This option is very useful when frequently exporting your scene is necessary but you have not changed your images. It's also useful if you modify the images outside of Unity and you do not want the exporter to delete your changes.

Lastly, the UV set option defaults to "Export First UV Set," which is the texture mapping used for diffuse textures. This version of this exporter only exports diffuse materials, so the other UV sets in the other choice in this menu, "All Three UV Sets," will be needed only if you know how to use the extra information in the application that will import the COLLADA document.

Animation Options

For the animation export, the first choice here is whether or not to export any animations. If you select "Animation export," the exporter will automatically bake matrices in the scene and export animations as 4x4 matrices. The animation clips options can be set to "Export All Clips" or "Export Single Clip," as shown in Figure 8-6. If "Export All Clips" is selected, all the animation curves will be stored at successive times, and the correct animation_clip information with begin and end times for each clip will be exported. If the importer does not support the clip information, the different animations will simply appear to be playing continuously one after another. See the single key section for instructions on exporting just a single clip.

Figure 8-6. *Animated character from Angry Bots game*

As for the evaluate frames option, the default is "Export All Animation Frames," which will export one matrix per frame of animation. If you select "Export Animation Keys," only the matrices at keyframes will be exported. This option should be used only if the software into which you want to import your COLLADA document is able to interpolate the values between the keyframes.

The single key option defaults to "Eliminate Single Key Animation." This is included because Unity allows single key animation in clips that would freeze the animation to the value in that key.

If "Export Single Clip" is selected, an additional parameter appears: "Name of Clip to Export." To be sure that you get only that animation, you must type the name of the clip exactly as it appears in the Unity animation clip selector. For example, a character that has "idle," "run," and "walk" animation clips can be exported with just the "run" animation. This option is there because several tools and the COLLADA importer do not support the animation_clip information.

In terms of the animation target, COLLADA allows for "Multiple Targets Per Clip" in order to keep the document small by sharing animation across multiple instanced objects (a.k.a. prefabs). Unfortunately, we found out that most COLLADA importers do not support multiple targets per clip; therefore you can select the option "Duplicate Animation Clips," which is a work-around but note that it bloats the size of the exported document.

For the export skins option, the default value is "Export Skins As Controllers," which is how skins and bones are expressed in COLLADA. If "Animation export" is selected, the animation will be applied to the bones through the controllers. Another option here is to "Export Skins as Geometry," which will convert the skins and bones to basic geometry (without the bone animation). This is useful when you want to export the model into an application that does not recognize skinning. The last choice is "Not Export Skins," which will completely ignore skinned objects in the export.

Terrain Options

For the terrain export, you may decide to export or not export the terrain information. If you do export the terrain, you can export or not export the trees attached to that terrain (see the trees option).

Another option is the sampling multiplier. Unity terrain data is very specific to the way it is implemented. Namely, a terrain is a height map associated with a Splat Map that contains up to four values (stored in a RGBA image) that are interpreted by the algorithm to blend between different materials (splat prototypes). The COLLADA Exporter creates a triangle mesh model of the terrain geometry with a density defined by the Sampling multiplier. Two triangles are created per quad, the corners of which correspond to each value in the HeightMap. So a 100x100 HeightMap will define 99*99 quads, resulting in 19,602 triangles. Using a multiplier of 0.25, the number of triangles will be INT(99*0.25) * INT(99*0.25) * 2 = 1728 triangles.

As for texture choices, the options for the diffuse material on export are defined by the texture choices parameter. "Single UV Approximation" is the default choice that assigns each triangle with the most important (greater coefficient in the Splat Map) material.

Figure 8-7 provides a good visual approximation of the terrain as rendered in Unity. The current limitation is that it only creates one UV set that is scaled by the "size" of the first splat prototype. If different sizes are used in the terrain, the textures other than the first one will have incorrect scale. Since the image is only an approximation of the visual terrain, it may be sufficient anyway, but please contact us if you find out you need something different. The other options are not to export any texture, or to export the Splat Map that covers the terrain. This is probably the most valuable option as it enables the user to use or modify the blending coefficients. The prototype textures will also be exported, but won't be attached to the terrain.

Figure 8-7. *A sample Unity terrain rendering*

Miscellaneous Options

Unity offers the option to fix names to valid XML. This option enables the exporter to save the names as is in the COLLADA document. By default, the names are converted to be valid XML name strings so the exported document will validate against the COLLADA schema. This restriction of the COLLADA 1.4.1 schema has been lifted in 1.5, but some applications will not be able to load a COLLADA document when names are not correctly XML-encoded.

The "bake matrix" option is only available if "Do Not Export Animation" has been selected. It allows the option to "Separate Rotation Translation And Scale" in the COLLADA scene.

The camera export option specifies whether or not to export the cameras. This is useful for tools such as Preview that enable the end user to have preset views.

The light export option allows you to specify whether to export the lights. Most of the time, it is recommended not to export the lights as many applications can only handle a very limited number of lights; otherwise, the scene may display as completely black with too many lights! Thus, it is probably best to rely on the lights of the importing application, such as Apple Preview.

The lightmaps export option enables you to "Export Lightmaps," which will copy the images used for lightmapping into the texture folder. Since this exporter only supports diffuse textures, the lightmaps won't appear in the importing application unless you write your own shaders (and export the secondary UV set, which contains the information needed for the lightmapping).

Exporting

The last button is Export, as shown in Figure 8-8, which is at the very bottom of the Exporter's dialog box (shown above in Figure 8-4).

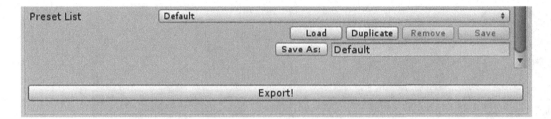

Figure 8-8. *The COLLADA Exporter Export button*

Once you click Export, as shown in Figure 8-8, it allows you to select where you want to export the COLLADA (.dae) document and texture folder.

Conclusion

The namespace COLLADA_1_4 containing the class COLLADA has been automatically generated by using xsd.exe, with a slightly modified COLLADA schema that can be obtained on the Khronos web site, http://khronos.org/collada. The direct link is www.khronos.org/files/collada_schema_1_4_1_ms.xsd.

If the COLLADA exporter is successful in the Asset Store, and/or we get feedback asking for additional features, we will add functionality to support shaders--particularly CgFX; add support for physics; and, time permitting, include JSON export for HTML5.

Questions? Send e-mail to contact@fl4re.com for more info!

PART 3

Web Tools

■ ■ ■

Introduction to Utilizing HTML, CSS, and JavaScript to Create Rich Debugging Information

Simon Franco

Often it is necessary while developing a game, or a tool, to create files to log the results of activities the application has performed. These log files record detailed information in order to help facilitate debugging. Once the application has finished running, the log files can be inspected by a programmer, or another user such as an artist, to help identify problems.

While these files are indispensable for the application's development, they are also sometimes very hard for a user to navigate through. They tend to be plain text, and the data they contain is often unorganized. That means that important information can be buried deep within them, making it difficult to find, or worse, easily missed.

This chapter presents a simple solution to this problem by leveraging advances in the field of web technologies.

Utilizing Web Technologies

With the continuous development of HTML[1] and other web technologies, we are given an opportunity to take advantage of advances in this area. The text-based nature of HTML, CSS, and JavaScript allows us to easily output an HTML file, along with any supporting JavaScript files, from our application as part of the log file generating process. This HTML log file can then be run within a web browser, where the data can be formatted, organized, and interpreted in a visual manner for the user. This organization and visualization of data allows the user to easily see how the application has performed, and to better spot problem areas without needing to skim through large quantities of text.

This article discusses some simple techniques and ideas for integrating these technologies into your game or tool.

---

[1]Berjon, Robin, Travis Leithead, Silvia Pfeiffer, Erika D. Navara, and Edward O'Connor. "HTML5: A vocabulary and associated APIs for HTML and XHTML." W3C. http://dev.w3.org/html5/spec/single-page.html.

Generating HTML Logs

Generating log files in HTML format after an application has performed its activities is fairly straightforward. You can easily categorize and store any interesting events in a list. You then iterate through each category and write out that category's events to an HTML file before the application terminates.

However, most of your logs will need to be written out while your game or tool is running. This is often essential; you frequently need to gather incremental information on your application, especially when it crashes before completing its task. Therefore, you must write out your HTML file in such a way that it remains valid after each written update. This requirement makes it necessary to implement a method of ensuring that the HTML tags you create are always correctly terminated.

A simple solution is to create a class that keeps a stack of the terminating HTML tags. When you create a new starting tag, you must push the corresponding terminating tag on to your stack and make a note of its length. Once you are finished filling in data for the tag, you write out the tag and then remove the corresponding terminating tag from the stack.

Every time you append HTML data to your currently open tags, you must first seek to the end of the HTML file, minus the combined text size of your stacked terminating tags. You then write out the new data to the file and then write out all the terminating tags contained within your stack.

For example, say you are writing out a simple table logging all asserts that fired while running a game. You want to add a new row to your table every time an assert fires. Therefore, you will write the following to your log file when you start the game, as shown in Listing 9-1.

Listing 9-1. Creating a Simple HTML Template for Your Log

```
<HTML>
  <HEAD>
    Our game's run-time assert log
  </HEAD>
  <BODY>
    <TABLE>
    </TABLE>
  </BODY>
</HTML>
```

As you are going to be generating data for the `<TABLE>` tag, you will still have the preceding HTML, BODY, and TABLE tags left non-terminated. Therefore, you will have pushed onto your stack the `</HTML>`, `</BODY>`, and `</TABLE>` terminating tags.

When writing out a new row of data for the table, you must first seek to the start of the `</TABLE>` tag. You then write the new table row, and then rewrite the terminating `</TABLE>`, `</BODY>`, and `</HTML>` tags. This approach ensures that the file always remains valid.

While exploring all the available HTML tags is beyond the scope of this chapter, I will briefly touch on a few tags I have found to be particularly useful.

TABLE

The TABLE tag provides you with the simplest way to organize the data being logged by your application. You can treat each table row as an item of generated information, such as the details of a triggered assert, or the name of a tested checkpoint from an auto-run of the game.

IMG

The IMG tag allows you to embed images directly into your log. This capability is particularly useful when you want to show statically generated graphical data from the game, such as a screenshot. This can be very useful during automated runs of the game. If an area of the game contains an unacceptable drop in frame rate, then you can have the game write out the frame buffer as an image file and add an IMG link to that file within the log.

CANVAS

This new tag provides you with a method to render graphical information in real time. You can use the canvas tag to render bar graphs and other charts to help visualize information about your game. This tag is one of the most exciting additions within the emerging HTML 5 standard.[2] With the ability to draw simple primitives, and by using JavaScript, you are able to dynamically create images representing game data. For example, you can interpret data from the game, such as a navigation mesh, and render it as a series of lines and shapes to show how it has been constructed, and to show any broken links between nodes.

Improving Log Readability with CSS

You've seen how to easily construct an HTML file while your application is running. By itself, this tool will help to organize your logged data, but with CSS,[3] you are able to drastically improve the readability and formatting of the log.

CSS allows you to stylize and format your logs. This has some immediate benefits, such as improving table readability by alternating row colors, highlighting problematic entries within a table, and generally structuring your page into a more visually pleasing form. As a simple introduction to CSS, Listing 9-2 shows a simple extracted piece of CSS script to style a sample HTML table.

Listing 9-2. Simple CSS to Style a Table

```
<HTML>
<HEAD>
<!-- Simple style setup for odd and event table rows -->
<style type="text/css">
    tr.odd { background-color:#CCCCCC }
    tr.even { background-color:#EEEEEE }
    tr.problem { background-color:#EE2020 }
    table.report_log { margin-left: auto; margin-right: auto;
                border-style:solid; border-width:1px;
                border-color:#222222;
                    background-color:#222222}
</style>
</HEAD>
<BODY>
<!-- Now populate our table -->
<TABLE class = "report_log">
    <tr class = "even"><td> 1st result </td></tr>
```

---

[2]Berjon, Robin, Travis Leithead, Silvia Pfeiffer, Erika D. Navara, and Edward O'Connor. "The CANVAS element." W3C. http://dev.w3.org/html5/spec/single-page.html#the-canvas-element.

[3]Bos, Bert. "Cascading Style Sheets." W3C. www.w3.org/Style/CSS/Overview.en.html.

```
        <tr class = "odd"><td> 2nd result </td></tr>
        <tr class = "problem">
            <td> Problematic 3rd result</td></tr>
        <tr class = "odd"><td> 4th result </td></tr>
</TABLE>
</BODY>
</HTML>
```

In Listing 9-2, you alternate the class of your table rows as they are being written out. You define a red background for problematic entries and set this as the table row class of any entry you want to alert the user to. See Figure 9-1 for a simple visualization of Listing 9-2.

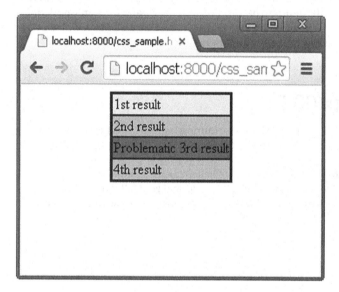

Figure 9-1. *A CSS coloring sample*

CSS gives you the functionality to make a log more manageable for users by providing custom views and more navigable by replacing plain text with formatted information. A simple way to do this would be to change the `display` property of an element to `none` when styling an element. This approach allows you to hide chunks of a log.

Your CSS styling data can either be written out as part of the HTML log or stored as a separate file. By storing the CSS data as a separate file on the user's machine, you can use it as a configuration file that specifies which data to include and how to display it.

Intelligent Reporting and Interactivity with JavaScript

Using HTML and CSS allows you to create richly formatted logs. However, by adding JavaScript, you open up the possibilities for intelligent reporting and interactivity.

JSON

Rather than having your application log all of its progress directly to an HTML file, you can instead have your application write a lightweight HTML log file during startup. Then you have each system log its activities to a separate JSON[4] file. JSON (JavaScript Object Notation) is a means of defining a JavaScript object with a set of keys and values. This simple file format allows for easy interchange of data between applications and web services.[5]

In your HTML file you use another piece of JavaScript to parse your JSON log files and appropriately add their data to the HTML page. You update your JavaScript log files using a similar method to how you originally updated your HTML log file. When you create a new object or array, you push the appropriate closing symbol onto the stack. To update the JavaScript file for a system, you must first seek to the end of the file, minus the string length of your closing symbol stack. You can then write the update, followed by writing out all the terminating symbols within your stack.

There are several advantages to logging applications' activity to JSON files. You can easily log processes that may be running concurrently (as they now have their own JSON file). Also, as your log data is separate from your log presentation, you can use the same JSON data within other logs. For example, you may wish to store the files as part of an archive so that you can compare log data from several sessions.

The other advantage of exporting your log data to JSON objects is that you can take advantage of numerous third-party libraries to manipulate JSON data in other languages4. This allows you to take log data and feed it back into the game or application. For example, if you have a JSON file that has logged un-freed memory allocations, then you can have the application break when that un-freed memory is being allocated. This allows the log data to feed back into the application's debugging.

As you have written JavaScript data, as opposed to raw HTML tags, you can perform some operations on the data before you convert it into HTML. For example, Listing 9-3 and Listing 9-4 show a brief demonstration sorting a memory log JSON file into a report. The program sorts the data in order of memory allocation size, so that the largest memory allocation is shown at the top of the table. It also contains a text box to allow the user to optionally enter a size threshold. Any memory allocations below this threshold will become hidden in the table. See Figure 9-2 for a visualization of this example.

Listing 9-3. Report.html Organizing Logged JavaScript Data

```
<HTML>
  <HEAD>
    <style type="text/css">
      tr.odd { background-color:#CCCCCC }
      tr.even { background-color:#EEEEEE }
      tr.off { display:none; }
      #report_table{background-color:#FFFFFF; padding: 2px;
      border-color:#333333; border-style:solid;
      border-width:2px; margin-left: auto;
      margin-right: auto }
    </style>
  </HEAD>

<script type="text/javascript">

  // Function called to initially populate the table.
  function generate_table()
```

4"Introducing JSON." www.json.org/.
5"JSON: The Fat-Free Alternative to XML." www.json.org/xml.html.

```javascript
{
  var request = new XMLHttpRequest();
  request.open('GET', './JSMemoryLog.json', false);
  request.overrideMimeType("application/json");
  request.send(null);

  var mem_log_array_json_data =
                      JSON.parse(request.responseText);
  var mem_log_array =
                  mem_log_array_json_data.memory_used;
  var report_table =
              document.getElementById("report_table_body");

  var sorted_table = new Array();

  // First sort the list.
  for ( var item in mem_log_array )
  {
    var entry = mem_log_array[ item ];
    var placed = false;
    for ( var sorted_item in sorted_table )
    {
      var sorted_entry = sorted_table[sorted_item];

      if ( entry.value > sorted_entry.value )
      {
        sorted_table.splice( sorted_item,0,entry );
        placed = true;
        break;
      }
    }
    if ( placed == false )
    {
      sorted_table.push( entry );
    }
  }

  // Add the sorted list elements to the table.
  for ( var item in sorted_table )
  {
   var entry = sorted_table[ item ];
   var row = document.createElement("tr");
   row.className = (item % 2 == 0) ? "even" : "odd";
   var column_data =  document.createElement("td");

   column_data.appendChild(document.createTextNode( entry.label ) );
   row.appendChild( column_data );

   column_data = document.createElement("td");
   column_data.appendChild(document.createTextNode( entry.value ) );
   row.appendChild( column_data );
   report_table.appendChild( row );
  }
}
```

```
    // Function called when the user updates the threshold.
    function update_report()
    {
     var threshold_text_box =
           document.getElementById("threshold_textinput");

     var threshold =  Number( threshold_text_box.value );
     var shown_row_id = 0;

     if ( threshold != "NaN" )
     {
       var report_table =
                 document.getElementById("report_table_body");

        for( var row_index = 1; row_index <
           report_table.rows.length; row_index++)
        {
          var row = report_table.rows[row_index];
          var value = Number(row.cells[1].innerHTML);

          if ( value < threshold )
          {
            row.className = "off";
          }
          else
          {
            row.className =
                (shown_row_id % 2 == 0) ? "even" : "odd";
            ++shown_row_id;
          }
        }
      }
     }
    }

  </script>

  <BODY onload = "generate_table();" >

    Threshold: <input type="text" name="threshold_textinput"
                                  id="threshold_textinput" />

    <input type="button" value="Filter" onclick = "update_report()"/>

    <table id = "report_table">
      <tbody id = "report_table_body">
        <tr>
          <td>System</td>
          <td>Mem used</td>
        </tr>
      </tbody>
    </table>
  </BODY>
</HTML>
```

Listing 9-4. JSMemoryLog.json – Logged Allocations from the Game

```json
{"memory_used":
  [
            {  "label" : "Textures",   "value" : 10.0 },
                { "label" : "Models",   "value" : 20.0 },
                { "label" : "Particle",   "value" : 5.0 },
                { "label" : "Characters",   "value" : 50.0 },
                { "label" : "Geometry",   "value" : 120.0 },
                { "label" : "Collision",   "value" : 50.0 },
                { "label" : "Sound",   "value" : 30.0 },
                { "label" : "Scripts",  "value" : 10.0 },
                { "label" : "Animation",  "value" : 25.0 }
  ]
}
```

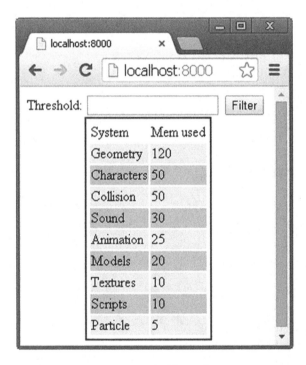

Figure 9-2. *A memory threshold visualization*

More on JavaScript: Live Reporting with AJAX

Statically reporting on the data generated by an application once it has completed is a very useful feature. However, with some applications, you will be interested in the data generated by the application before it has completed its process. To do this, you can make use of AJAX (Asynchronous JavaScript and XML).[6]

---

[6]van Kesteren, Anne. "XMLHttpRequest Level 2." W3C. www.w3.org/TR/XMLHttpRequest/.

To utilize AJAX, you will need to change your XMLHttpRequest to be processed asynchronously. You must also change how your data is read; instead of a single read request when your page is loaded, you read your JSON file at regular intervals and then update your log's display accordingly. You can do this using the JavaScript setInterval function to reissue a read request sometime after your last one has completed.

Once the read has completed, you can regenerate the part of your log that you want to be updated live. This allows your logs to update while the application is running. A example of this can be seen in Listing 9-5 where you replace the generate_table function in order to refresh the data every two seconds. You also remove the generate_table(); function call in the onload parameter for the BODY tag. It is worth noting that for the asynchronous functionality to work, you may have to run an HTTP server for the JSON file serving to function. This can be done easily by using WAMP[7] or Python.[8]

Listing 9-5. Modified generate_table Function from Report.html

```
setInterval( function generate_table()
{
        var request = new XMLHttpRequest();
        request.open('GET', './JSMemoryLog.json', true);
        request.overrideMimeType("application/json");
        request.onload = function(e) {
                var mem_log_array_json_data =
                                JSON.parse(request.responseText);
                var mem_log_array =

                mem_log_array_json_data.memory_used;
                var report_table =
                                document.getElementById("report_table_body");
                while (report_table.childNodes.length >2)
                {
                        report_table.removeChild(report_table.lastChild);
                }
                var sorted_table = new Array();

                // First sort the list.
                for ( var item in mem_log_array )
                {
                    var entry = mem_log_array[ item ];
                    var placed = false;
                    for ( var sorted_item in sorted_table )
                    {
                        var sorted_entry = sorted_table[sorted_item];
                        if ( entry.value > sorted_entry.value )
                        {
                                sorted_table.splice( sorted_item,0,entry );
                                placed = true;
                                break;
                        }
                }
```

---

[7]wampserver, "WAMPSERVER, a Windows web development environment." www.wampserver.com/en/.
[8]Python.org, "20.19. SimpleHTTPServer — Simple HTTP request handler."
https://docs.python.org/2/library/simplehttpserver.html.

```
                    }
                    if ( placed == false )
                    {
                            sorted_table.push( entry );
                    }
                }
            // Add the sorted list elements to the table.
             for ( var item in sorted_table )
             {
                var entry = sorted_table[ item ];
                var row = document.createElement("tr");
                row.className = (item % 2 == 0) ? "even" : "odd";
                var column_data =  document.createElement("td");

                column_data.appendChild(document.createTextNode( entry.label ));
                row.appendChild( column_data );
                column_data = document.createElement("td");
                column_data.appendChild(document.createTextNode(entry.value));
                row.appendChild( column_data );
                report_table.appendChild( row );
                update_report();
             }
        }
        request.send(null);
}, 2000 );
```

Visualizing Data

Using the canvas element, you are able to visually represent data to help make information within the log more accessible. Being able to graphically represent logged data is one of the strengths of generated HTML logs. You now have the ability to extrapolate data from multiple sources to create visualizations tailored to the interests of the user viewing the report.

For example, when rendering your navigation mesh, you can easily add the option to highlight nodes where a character has spent time idling, or died. These can be color-coded to help highlight areas where characters may be getting trapped, or where there may be difficulty spikes.

As mentioned previously, canvas is one of the most powerful HTML elements. However, if these logs are being used internally, then you may take advantage of technologies that may not be implemented in every browser, such as WebGL.[9] WebGL is based on OpenGL ES 2.0[10] and so offers many opportunities to render complex 3D data.

Other Third-Party JavaScript Libraries

By using standard web technologies, you can leverage the vast wealth of free and open source software to enrich your logs. While delving into each of these is beyond the scope of this chapter, I will present a short list of useful libraries to investigate.

---

[9]The Khronos Group. "WebGL - OpenGL ES 2.0 for the Web." www.khronos.org/webgl/.
[10]The Khronos Group. "OpenGL ES 2_X - The Standard for Embedded Accelerated 3D Graphics." www.khronos.org/opengles/2_X/.

jQuery

jQuery[11] is a popular library that helps simplify AJAX queries and HTML document manipulation. jQuery is particularly useful if you need to support multiple browsers for your logs and reduces the amount of boilerplate code that needs to be written.

Flotr2

Flotr2[12] is a simple library module for creating graphs. It is especially useful for log writing when manual implementation of graph rendering would be time-consuming. The advantage to creating graphs with JavaScript is that they can be updated in real time to reflect changes to the dataset and user requirements.

Conclusion

There are many opportunities made available to us by these constantly developing web technologies. It is worth noting, however, that due to legacy browsers, and some browser incompatibility issues, some features may require either additional CSS attributes or code workarounds to ensure that your logs are displayed in a similar manner across the browsers you wish to support. There are various free resources available to help identify features which may be incompatible on certain web browsers.[13]

---

[11]The jQuery Foundation. "jQuery, write less, do more." `http://jquery.com/`.
[12]Humble Software Development. "flotr2." `http://humblesoftware.com/flotr2/`.
[13]Can I use… "Compatibility tables for support of HTML5, CSS3, SVG and more in desktop and mobile browsers." `www.caniuse.com`.

CHAPTER 10

■ ■ ■

Moving Tools to the Cloud: Control, Configure, Monitor, and View Your Game with WebSocket

John McCutchan

Your engine needs great tools because they increase developer and artist productivity. Engine tools will automate tasks such as baking assets or regression testing, but they're not just for automation; they are also companion applications that allow you to control, configure, monitor, and view your engine.

At the highest level, engine tools can be split into two categories: tools that communicate directly with an engine while it is running, and tools that run independent of the engine. Examples of the latter include mesh bakers and graphics shader compilers. Tools that communicate with the engine are companion applications running along or inside the game engine. A dynamic graph showing the amount of memory presently allocated, a Quake-style command console, and property panels for configuring game objects are examples of companion tools. This chapter focuses on companion tools.

Often embedded inside the running game, companion tools have the benefits of being synchronized and in control of the game engine, but they suffer from a few problems. First of all, they require a GUI framework that can run inside the game. Off-the-shelf GUI frameworks exist, but they often come with large dependencies or inappropriate licenses, or they conflict with the game itself. Second, because companion tools run as part of the engine, there can be long iteration times. A minor change to the tool, such as adding a toggle button, requires that the game be recompiled, relinked, and restarted, incurring the cost of reloading all assets needed to run it. A third problem with companion tools is that console development kits do not have a mouse or keyboard, relegating the UI to harder-to-use input methods like analog sticks, D-pads, and onscreen keyboards. Finally, by coupling the tools to the game instance itself, a developer must be sitting next to the development hardware in order to use them.

Moving these tools out of the game engine and into web applications solves or avoids these problems and gives you a great platform for developing tools. Browsers are ideal for creating rich GUIs with very fast iteration times. Because the tools are browser applications, they are remotely accessible. They're also easy to distribute because they contain no dependencies other than the browser itself. More important, building the tools as web applications that communicate over the network with an instance of the engine requires a clear separation between tools and the game, with the benefit of cleaner design and a more modular code base.

Web applications are generally considered to be synonymous with "the cloud," which means that both they and the data they use reside on multiple remote servers accessible via a web browser.

Figure 10-1 shows the separation between the tools and the game communicating via network messages.

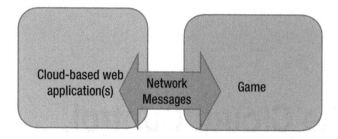

Figure 10-1. *Separation of game and tools communicating over the network*

Recently, the browser has evolved from being a tool for viewing web sites to an ideal platform for building desktop-quality applications. Browser vendors have adopted HTML5, WebSocket, and WebGL, and are quickly filling in the missing pieces such as gamepad support and mouse locking (needed for first person shooter mouse controls).

The rest of this chapter will present a foundation for building engine tools as browser applications, offer sample applications, and provide technical details involved in building a WebSocket server and JSON-based remote procedure call system.

Foundation

My proposal is to construct an API for engine tools (ET-API), built on a remote procedure call system using JSON for data encoding and the recently standardized WebSocket protocol for network transmission. The tools will run in a browser, so it is important that ET-API is easy to use from there. This section of the chapter will provide concrete definitions of RPC, JSON, WebSocket, etc., while laying a foundation for moving engine tools to the cloud.

What exactly is a remote procedure call system? Simply put, it is a function call from one process to another. The processes do not have to be running on the same machine or share the same architecture. When attempting to understand RPC, it is helpful to first consider a local procedure call in a language like C/C++. When a local procedure call occurs, the arguments are pushed onto the stack, then the program branches to the address of the function being called. When the called function returns, the result is stored on the stack for the calling function to access. This procedure call mechanism works because the caller, callee, and shared data live in the same address space and agree on calling conventions that make use of the shared address space. In a remote procedure call system, the caller, callee, and data do not share an address space and thus cannot share data by memory address. In other words, the calling convention for a remote procedure call system must define not only how arguments are passed and returned, but also the format the arguments are encoded in. In order to make a remote procedure call, you must marshal (encode) the parameters for transmission over the network and pack them into a message for the remote system. Once the message has been prepared, it is transported to the remote process. The return value(s) from an RPC are sent in a similar manner but in the opposite direction.

Because the tools will be running inside a browser, it is important that you pick a data encoding scheme that is native to the browser. I've chosen JavaScript Object Notation (JSON) data encoding. (JSON is text-only data encoding that every browser can serialize JavaScript objects into and construct JavaScript objects from.) The primitive types are the keywords null, true, and false, as well as decimal numbers and strings. In addition to the primitive types, JSON has two collections. The first collection is an unordered key/value map. The second collection is an ordered list (or array). Listing 10-1 shows some sample JSON from a player profile.

Listing 10-1. Some JSON from a Player Profile

```
{
    "PlayerName" : "John McCutchan",
    "RecentScores" : [10000, 12345, 99, 1, 0],
    "TrophyList": [
        { "TrophyName": "5 in a row", "Unlocked": false },
        { "TrophyName": "First Timer", "Unlocked": true }
    ]
}
```

The special characters { and } begin and end a key/value map. The special characters [and] begin and end an ordered list. In Listing 10-1, the root keys are PlayerName, RecentScores, and TrophyList. The value of the TrophyList key is an ordered list of trophies, each having a TrophyName and an Unlocked flag.

Aside from being the native data structure of browser applications, JSON is easily read and written by humans with far less markup than, for example, XML.

Now that the data-marshaling format has been fixed, the next piece of the ET-API puzzle is the RPC message framing, that is, the mandatory portion of the RPC message. Each RPC is a JSON map with two required keys: the message type and the message serial number or ID, as shown in Listing 10-2.

Listing 10-2. The Message Type and the Message ID

```
{
    "type" : "<type>"
    "id" : "<id>"
}
```

The type field is used to indicate the type of message. ET-API supports three types: command, result, and report. I will explain each of these shortly.

The ID field is used to pair related messages together. For example, the command shown in Listing 10-3 has an ID of 4.

Listing 10-3. The ID Field Pairs Related Messages Together.

```
{
    "type" : "command",
    "id" : "4",
    ...
}
```

The result of the command sent back from the engine to the browser application will also have an ID of 4. This ID makes connecting a function call and return value easy.

Returning to the type field, the possibilities are

- Command: Commands initiate some sort of action or state change.

- Result: The result of a command. Linked together with the id field. Commands are not required to reply with a result.

- Report: A regular, repeating message from a subscription. Clients can subscribe to report channels and set an interval between reports.

All other fields in a message are dictated by the requirements of the command. ET-API has three stock commands:

- Echo: Results in a reply message containing a copy of the message key.

- Subscribe: Caller is subscribed to a report channel.

- Unsubscribe: Caller is unsubscribed from a report channel.

The final piece of the ET-API foundation is the transmission and reception of messages over the network between the browser application and the game engine. ET-API could have used HTTP, but browsers now support a much more efficient network protocol, WebSocket. WebSocket is a communication protocol that allows for bidirectional text and binary message passing. Think TCP for the browser. The WebSocket protocol is very bandwidth efficient (message framing is at most 14 bytes), and the payloads are custom to the application. Since a WebSocket connection is only a thin layer on top of TCP, the latency is low, too.

Examples

With the ET-API foundation in place, I will introduce tools that were created with ET-API. This section will cover sample applications that include asset preview, live monitoring, live editing, remote viewing, and unit testing.

My engine allows for browser tools to preview three asset classes: textures, meshes, and models. Models are a combination of textures, meshes, and shaders. I have not considered audio preview.

The way the tools preview each type of asset is essentially the same. The tool sends a command requesting a specific asset, and the engine sends the asset over as a result. Once the tool receives the asset data, it caches the data locally so the network traffic is minimal. How the asset data is packed depends on the asset class. For a mesh, the index buffer and associated vertex buffers must be sent over. This mesh data is then loaded into WebGL index and vertex buffer objects. For a texture, each slice of the mipmap pyramid must be sent over. Once the entire mipmap pyramid is in the browser, the preview tool can display the texture at each level of detail and overlay texture coordinates on top using the browser canvas.

Live performance monitoring tools are fed data by a reporter. The browser tool subscribes to a reporter and sets an update frequency. Figure 10-2 shows a report from the MemoryGraph reporter.

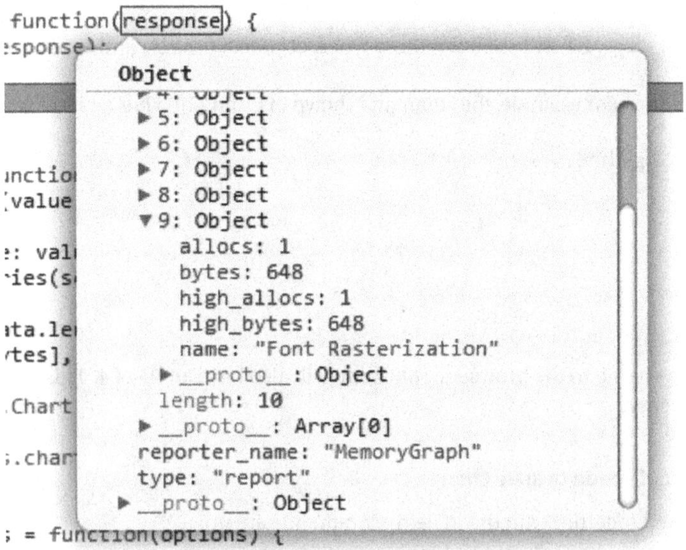

Figure 10-2. *A sample message from the MemoryGraph reporter*

Each MemoryGraph report includes an array of allocators. For each allocator, the current number of allocations and bytes allocated is included along with the high water mark of each. Figure 10-3 displays this data with a live graph.

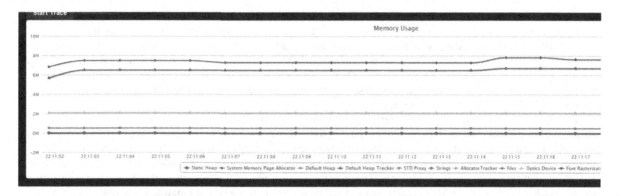

Figure 10-3. *Graph of memory usage over time*

Live editing is made possible by making all game objects and their properties uniquely identifiable. Once you have this system in place, creating new objects or updating existing objects' properties becomes a matter of issuing simple commands. For live editing, the appropriate user interface is very game-specific.

A remote viewer tool captures the output from the running game and displays it in the browser. A remote viewer can be taken a step further by having the browser tool send user input back to the engine. My remote viewer application is very simple. The browser tool requests a screenshot from the engine, and after receiving a screenshot, asks for another. By having the request for an updated screenshot come from the browser tool, you don't force the engine to produce and send more frames than the network can handle. This client request is a very simple form of rate limiting. Figure 10-4 shows the display from a toy demo rendering a tessellated wireframe teapot.

Figure 10-4. *Screenshot of remote viewer*

It may be hard to make out, but the image is encoded at about 50% JPEG quality and is running at about 20 frames per second. The engine frame buffer was 960 x 540 pixels, and encoding it as a JPEG took about three milliseconds. At medium quality, I was easily able to obtain 30 frames per second with "good enough" image quality. This type of remote viewer requires a large amount of bandwidth. Each frame amounted to about 64 KiB of JPEG data. Running at 30 frames per second, the tool needs 1920 KiB per second. This bandwidth requirement is fine for a local area network (even a WiFi one) but is inappropriate for streaming over the Internet. For reference, the engine was running single-threaded on an Intel Core i5 CPU.

Various forms of testing are possible with an ET-API system. You can do regression testing, for example, by capturing performance data such as memory used. Each day, the engine can be spawned, and a remote browser can create a fixed set of objects while observing total memory used. If this total amount has changed, the tool can notify developers of a potential memory leak. Testing the renderer becomes possible with the remote viewing capabilities. On each test run, the browser tool constructs a scene, places the camera, and requests a screenshot. This screenshot is compared with a previously approved screenshot. If they do not match, a bug may have been introduced into the renderer.

Technical Details

Implementing ET-API for your engine requires a WebSocket server, a system for managing multiple connections, report generators, and command processors. This section will cover each of these in turn.

The WebSocket Protocol

A WebSocket connection begins life as a regular HTTP connection. The connection is upgraded from HTTP to WebSocket. This upgrade is one-way; you can't revert back to an HTTP connection. Listing 10-4 shows a sample upgrade request.

Listing 10-4. A Sample Upgrade Request

```
GET /servicename HTTP/1.1
Host: server.example.com
Upgrade: websocket
Connection: Upgrade
Sec-WebSocket-Key: dGhlIHNhbXBsZSBub25jZQ==
Origin: http://example.com
```

Listing 10-5 shows how the server responds.

Listing 10-5. Server Response to an Upgrade Request

```
HTTP/1.1 101 Switching Protocols
Upgrade: websocket
Connection: Upgrade
Sec-WebSocket-Accept: s3pPLMBiTxaQ9kYGzzhZRbK+xOo=
```

Most of these HTTP fields are self-explanatory, but not Sec-WebSocket-Key and Sec-WebSocket-Accept. Sec-WebSocket-Key is a string sent by the client as a challenge to the server. The challenge is there so that the client is sure that it is communicating with an actual (and up-to-date) WebSocket server. This example leads to the question, how does the server calculate the value of Sec-WebSocket-Accept and complete the challenge? The answer is quite simple. The server first takes Sec-WebSocket-Key and concatenates it with a GUID string from the WebSocket specification. Then the SHA-1 hash of the resulting string is computed, and finally, Sec-WebSocket-Accept is the base64 encoding of the hash value. Let's work through an example, starting with Listing 10-6.

Listing 10-6. The Connection is Upgraded to WebSocket

```
SpecifcationGUID = "258EAFA5-E914-47DA-95CA-C5AB0DC85B11";
FullWebSocketKey = concatenate(Sec-WebSocket-Key, SpecifcationGUID);
-> dGhlIHNhbXBsZSBub25jZQ==258EAFA5-E914-47DA-95CA-C5AB0DC85B11
KeyHash = SHA-1(FullWebSocketKey);
-> 0xb3 0x7a 0x4f 0x2c 0xc0 0x62 0x4f 0x16 0x90 0xf6 0x46 0x06 0xcf 0x38 0x59 0x45 0xb2 0xbe 0xc4
0xea
Sec-Websocket-Accept = base64(KeyHash)
-> s3pPLMBiTxaQ9kYGzzhZRbK+xOo=
```

After the client has successfully completed the challenge, the connection is upgraded from HTTP to WebSocket and all communication must be performed through WebSocket.

Unlike TCP, WebSocket is a message-based protocol. No end of a WebSocket connection can receive a half-transmitted message. At the protocol level, each message begins with a header defining the length of the message, the type (text, binary, or control), and other metadata. The message payload immediately follows the message header. All incoming messages will include a 32-bit mask, which must be applied to the entire payload with an XOR operation. Each message will have a different mask.

The header begins with a 16-bit mask (light background) and up to 12 bytes of optional header (dark background) shown in Figure 10-5.

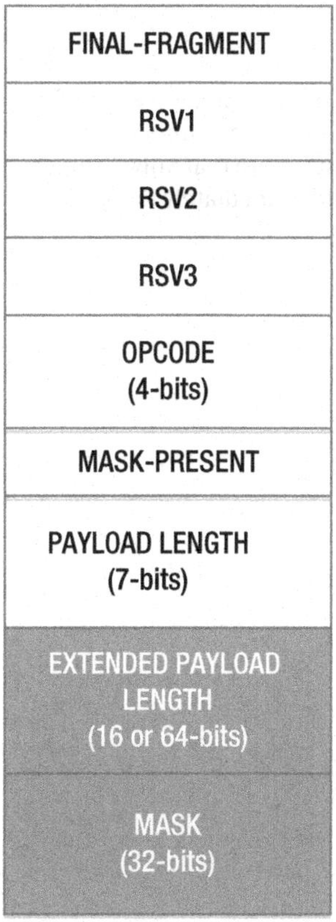

Figure 10-5. *WebSocket packet data layout*

The header mask indicates whether this packet is the final fragment of a message (messages can be split into fragments), what the opcode is, and whether a mask is present. The payload length field plays double duty. For small messages (less than 125 bytes), it holds the length of the message, but for messages that are longer, the payload length is used as a flag to indicate the size of the extended payload length field. The extended payload length follows immediately after the first 16 bits of the header (it comes before the mask). When payload length is equal to 126, the extended payload length is 16 bits, and when it is equal to 127, the extended payload length is 64 bits.

WebSocket opcodes are split into three categories: continuation, non-control, and control. Continuation and non-control opcodes indicate user messages, and control frames are used to configure the protocol itself. Presently the following opcodes are defined as shown in Table 10-1.

Table 10-1. *WebSocket Opcodes*

opcode	Meaning
0x0	Message continuation [continuation]
0x1	Text message [non-control]
0x2	Binary message [non-control]
0x8	Connection Close [control]
0x9	Ping [control]
0xA	Pong [control]

Once you have parsed the header, extracting the payload is trivial. Do not forget to XOR in the mask. Parsing the header is made interesting by the fact that its size and layout are variable and thus cannot be mapped directly to a C structure. However, because each WebSocket message is at least 16 bits, you can define a structure that only reserves 16 bits (a uint16_t) of storage, the optional header fields and payload of the message should immediately follow the header in memory, see Listing 10-7.

Listing 10-7. The WebSocketMessageHeader

```
struct WebSocketMessageHeader {
  union {
    struct {
      unsigned int OP_CODE : 4;
      unsigned int RSV1 : 1;
      unsigned int RSV2 : 1;
      unsigned int RSV3 : 1;
      unsigned int FIN : 1;
      unsigned int PAYLOAD : 7;
      unsigned int MASK : 1;
    } bits;
    uint16_t short_header;
};

  size_t GetMessageLength() const;
  size_t GetPayloadOffset() const;
  size_t GetPayloadLength() const;
  uint32_t GetMask() const;
```

```
uint8_t GetOpCode() const;
bool IsFinal() const;
bool IsMasked() const;

...

};
```

A WebSocketMessageHeader will always be at least 16 bits long, so the only data element defined inside the struct is short_header. Accessing the mask and extended payload lengths or the payload is done with an offset from &short_header. When I want to parse a header, I simply do this:

```
WebSocketMessageHeader* header = &buffer[i];
```

I have found this approach to be very clean; it is generally useful when dealing with structures that do not have a fixed length or layout.

Messages can be split into multiple fragments. When this happens, the FINAL-FRAGMENT bit will be zero until the final message. The first fragment will have the opcode indicating either a text (0x1) or binary (0x2) message, and the rest of the fragments will have the opcode of continuation (0x0).

The protocol supports ping (0x9) and pong (0xA) messages. When a ping message has a payload, the consequent pong message must have an identical payload. You are only required to pong the most recent ping if more than one ping arrives.

A WebSocket Server

Now that the WebSocket protocol is understood, I will describe the high-level design of my WebSocket server. My server uses three buffers: one for incoming WebSocket data, one for outgoing WebSocket data, and one to store fully parsed incoming messages. Listing 10-8 shows an outline of the API.

Listing 10-8. Outline of the WebSocket Server API

```
class WebSocketServer {
public:
 WebSocketServer();

 int AcceptConnection(TcpListener* listener);
 int CloseConnection();

 void Update();

 int SendTextMessage(const char* msg);
 int SendTextMessage(const char* msg, size_t msg_length);

 uint64_t PendingMessageCount() const;
 void ProcessMessages(OnMessageDelegate del, void* userdata);
 void ClearMessages();
};
```

■ **Note**   Some trivial methods have been omitted.

Listening for a connection over TCP must be decoupled from the WebSocket server itself. Each instance of WebSocketServer is responsible for only one client. This separation keeps the code and resource allocation simple. A higher-level system should manage multiple connection requests and multiple live WebSocket connections.

My WebSocket server has a single Update method. This method pumps the connection. It is responsible for sending any pending messages, receiving any new messages (ultimately moving them to the message buffer), and updating status flags (connection opened, connection closed, connection error).

Complete incoming messages are stored in their own buffer. When the engine system is ready to process incoming messages, a call to ProcessMessages is made and a delegate function is passed in. The WebSocketServer will iterate over all messages in the buffer and call this delegate for each one. When the engine is done with the messages, it must clear them by calling ClearMessages.

I started with the explicit goal of supporting multiple connected clients. I've discussed the importance of decoupling the code that waits for a connection over TCP from the code that manages a WebSocket connection. Because of that decoupling, supporting multiple connections is practically free.

Command Processing

Support for commands is added by implementing the commander interface, as shown in Listing 10-9.

Listing 10-9. Implementing the Commander Interface

```
class doCommandCenterCommanderInterface {
public:
 virtual const char* CommanderName() const = 0;
 virtual bool CanProcessCommand(const doCommandCenterCommandPacket* packet) const = 0;
 virtual void ProcessCommand(doCommandCenterConnection* connection, const
doCommandCenterCommandPacket* packet) = 0;
};
```

A commander can process one or many commands (CanProcessCommand). Each commander is registered with the central command center, which routes messages from connected clients to the appropriate commander. doCommandCenterCommandPacket just contains a parsed JSON object, and doCommandCenterConnection has the WebSocket connection and various buffers in it.

Support for reports is added by implementing the reporter interface, as shown in Listing 10-10.

Listing 10-10. Implementing the Reporter Interface

```
class doCommandCenterReporterInterface {
public:
    virtual const char* ReporterName() const = 0;
    // Update internal state
    virtual void Refresh() = 0;
    // Report state to all subscribed connections
    virtual void Report() = 0;
};
```

Each reporter is responsible for generating a single type of report. Similar to commanders, reporters are registered in the central command center.

Client commands to subscribe and unsubscribe are processed by a commander, like all other commands.

Future Work

There are many avenues for future work in browser-based tools. One possibility is a video streaming solution that makes more efficient use of bandwidth while minimizing the CPU load during encoding. It would be interesting to see the game engine and the game play completely isolated from each other. The game play code would use ET-API to remotely script the engine, although latency could make this difficult. Finally, I'd like to extend this approach to offline asset baking. The engine could be notified over ET-API when an asset is baked and could be reloaded.

Conclusion

I am proposing that your engine define an API for engine tools (ET-API). ET-API is exposed as a JSON-based remote procedure call sitting on top of the WebSocket protocol. With ET-API in place, all engine tools are built as browser applications. The engine should support multiple simultaneously connected tools. I have offered examples of a remote viewer, live editing, live performance monitoring, asset preview, and testing. Each of these applications can be cloud hosted, providing a central location for all tools used in a game studio. If these tools allow content to be created, players could be allowed access to them to create add-ons for the game. These examples are just the tip of the iceberg. Although much of this chapter has been devoted to exposing a game written in C/C++ to browser tools, this approach is applicable to game engines written in any language—even a game written for a web browser.

PART 4

Programming

CHAPTER 11

■ ■ ■

Programming: Decoupling Game Tool GUIs from Core Editing Operations

Nicuşor Nedelcu

Since the early days of video game development when the programmer had to write the code plus design and create the levels without the aid of a game editor, the tools to create games have evolved into the must-have game development software we use today. Now the level editors are built into the development kits, and the developer's job is much easier—but still filled with potential pitfalls.

In the past few years, it has become common to decouple game level editor operations and functionality from game-specific features, so that the editor can be reused for more games and game types. The same thing has happened on the game engine side: engines have become more and more flexible and reusable.

But problems remain. One big issue with game level editors is complexity and manageability. Once you have added many features to the editor, it will grow in source code size and complexity, and will become harder and harder to maintain and extend. Another problem is that you have to choose a GUI toolkit to create your interface. That can become a headache if you ever decide to switch to another GUI toolkit, since many editing operations are tied in with the UI code itself.

To address the issue of changing GUI toolkits in these fast and ever-shifting times, we present a method of decoupling the visual user interface code from the non-GUI editing operations code in the game level editor or other tools. By separating the UI from core editing functions, you can change to another GUI toolkit in no time, leaving the editing operations code almost untouched. The decoupling operation can be accomplished via C++ editor core functionality code and various editor user interfaces using GUI toolkits like Qt,[1] MS WinForms, WPF, MFC, HTML5/JavaScript, or even a command-line editor UI, all using the same editor functionality code as a common hub. Communication between the editor functions and the visual interface is achieved through a command system (basically the Command Pattern). We will also explore the architecture of a plug-in system using this command communication approach.

Editor Ecosystem

The editor is split into two major logical parts:

- **Non-visual:** Consisting of editor core, plug-ins, and their commands (no GUI).

- **Visual:** Created using the UI toolkit of your choice, which will call the commands provided by the plug-ins and editor core.

---

[1]Nokia. "Qt—Cross-platform application and UI framework." http://qt.nokia.com.

In Figure 11-1, you can see the entire editor ecosystem.

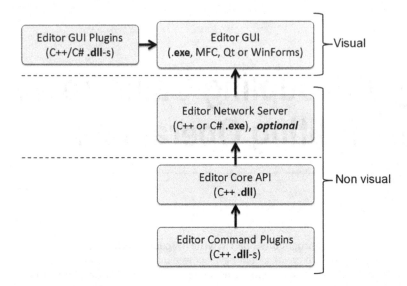

Figure 11-1. *The editor ecosystem*

The editor GUI can be developed using any UI SDK/API, and it can have its own plug-ins. For example, sub-editors like the model editor, cinematic editor, scene editor, material editor, etc., can be hosted by the main editor, and you can even run them as separate tools. Each tool will implement its own UI functionality and will call commands by their name and parameter values (arguments). The editor core will search its registered commands list and dispatch the call to the appropriate plug-in command.

You can also have an editor network layer, which waits for tools to connect to it and simply dispatches command calls and sends back their results. There are various other methods of communication between the GUI and the editor core; these methods use IPC (inter-process communication[2]) such as pipes, DDE, and shared memory or files, but sockets are supported on all platforms, so they are the obvious first choice.

Editor Core C++ API

Now let's get to the nuts and bolts of the actual code. First you will declare your editor C++ interface to be used by the plug-ins. You are going to expose plug-in and command methods and interfaces, a simple history (undo/redo) system, and an event system (used for triggering events in the editor, plug-ins can register themselves as event sinks to receive or trigger events).

Let's start with the building block interfaces related to commands, undo, events, and other primitive constructs. You will use a self-contained, independent header file, with only pure interfaces, not relying on external headers so it can be easily wrapped or converted to other languages. (It's especially important to keep the interfaces simple. If you were using something like SWIG (Simplified Wrapper and Interface Generator[3]), for example, having too many dependencies in the C++ code would complicate things for the SWIG converter, sometimes failing to properly create a wrapper for other languages.)

---

[2]"Inter-process communication." http://en.wikipedia.org/wiki/Inter-process_communication.
[3]"SWIG." http://en.wikipedia.org/wiki/SWIG.

After you define your simple types like uint32, you define a Handle union to be used as a pointer transporter between the calling application and the editor core internals. This will keep things simpler, since the user can't use the pointer itself anyway (see Listing 11-1).

Listing 11-1. A Generic Handle Container

```
// A generic handle, used to pass pointers in command parameters without having
// to know the pointer type
union Handle
{
   Handle()
      : hVoidPtr(NULL)
   {}
   explicit Handle(int32 aVal)
      : hInt(aVal)
   {}
   explicit Handle(int64 aVal)
      : hInt64(aVal)
   {}
   explicit Handle(void* pVal)
      : hVoidPtr(pVal)
   {}
   int32 hInt;
   int64 hInt64;
   void* hVoidPtr;
};
```

You will also need a Version structure to be used in the various version comparisons/validations you will have for the editor API and plug-in versions (see Listing 11-2).

Listing11-2. A Generic Version Holder Structure

```
// A version structure, holding version information for plug-in or editor
struct Version
{
   Version();
   Version(uint32 aMajor, uint32 aMinor, uint32 aBuild);
   bool operator <= (const Version& rOther) const;
   bool operator >= (const Version& rOther) const;
   Version& operator = (const char* pVerStr);

   uint32 major, minor, build;
};
```

After this, a central point of the editor core API is the main editor interface (see Listing 11-3), which will provide command, plug-in, and event methods to be used by plug-ins and their commands, and also by the main editor skeleton application, which will manage those plug-ins.

Listing 11-3. The Main Editor Core Interface

```cpp
// The editor main interface
struct IEditor
{
  enum ELogMsgType
  {
    eLogMsg_Info,
    eLogMsg_Debug,
    eLogMsg_Warning,
    eLogMsg_Error,
    eLogMsg_Fatal
  };

  virtual ~IEditor(){}
  virtual Version GetVersion() const = 0;
  virtual void PushUndoAction(IUndoAction* pAction) = 0;
  virtual bool CanUndo(uint32 aSteps = 1) = 0;
  virtual void Undo(uint32 aSteps = 1) = 0;
  virtual void Redo(uint32 aSteps = 1) = 0;
  virtual void ClearHistory(int32 aSteps = -1) = 0;
  virtual bool RegisterCommand(IPlugin* pPlugin,
                    TPfnCommand pCmdFunc,
                    const char* pCmdName) = 0;
  virtual bool UnregisterCommand(TPfnCommand pCmdFunc) = 0;
  virtual bool IsCommandRegistered(
                    const char* pCmdName) = 0;
  virtual bool RegisterEvent(IEvent* pEvent) = 0;
  virtual bool UnregisterEvent(IEvent* pEvent) = 0;
  virtual bool IsEventRegistered(
                    const char* pEventName) = 0;
  virtual bool TriggerEvent(IEvent* pEvent,
                    IEventSink::ETriggerContext aContext,
                    void* pUserData) = 0;
  virtual void CallEventSinks(IEvent* pEvent,
                    void* pUserData) = 0;
  virtual bool RegisterEventSink(
                    IEventSink* pEventSink) = 0;
  virtual bool UnregisterEventSink(
                    IEventSink* pEventSink) = 0;
  virtual IParameterValues* CreateParameterValues() = 0;
  virtual IParameterDefinitions*
              CreateParameterDefinitions() = 0;
  virtual bool Call(
                    const char* pCommandName,
                    IParameterValues* pParams) = 0;
  virtual void WriteLog(
                    ELogMsgType aType,
                    const char* pModule,
                    const char* pFormat, ...) = 0;
};
```

This is the main editor interface at a glance. Its methods are quite self-explanatory, the most used methods being the Call(...) method, which is used to execute commands by their name and requires a parameter "bag" (optional), and the IParameterValues interface, created before the call by the user using the CreateParameterValues() method and then filling up the parameter values for the command to use.

Plug-ins

The plug-ins are DLLs loaded by the core editor DLL. Each plug-in will expose and register its commands in the editor's ecosystem and provide information about these commands through a manifest file associated with the plug-in's DLL.

A core editor plug-in consists of two files:

- A C++ DLL file, the plug-in code (Example.dll)

- A manifest file (Example.plugin.xml[4]), having the same base file name as the plug-in's DLL (Example), containing information about it.

Listing 11-4 shows an example of a plug-in manifest file.

Listing 11-4. Plug-in Manifest File

```
<plugin
    name="Example"
    description="The example editor plugin"
    author="Nicusor Nastase Nedelcu"
    url="http://some.com"
    guid="31D91906-1125-4784-81FF-119C15267FC3"
    version="1.0.0"
    minEditorVersion="1.0.0"
    maxEditorVersion="2.0.0"
    icon="example.png"
    unloadable="true">
    <dependencies>
        <depends nameHint="OtherPlugin"
            guid="DAA91906-1125-4784-81FF-319C15267FC3" />
        <depends nameHint="SomeOtherPlugin"
            guid="F51A2113-1361-1431-A3EA-B4EA2134A111" />
    </dependencies>
    <commands>
        <command name="get_some_thing"
            info="This command get something">
            <param name="someParam1" type="int32"
                info="this is parameter 1" />
            <param name="someParam2" type="float"
                info="this is parameter 2" />
        </command>
    </commands>
</plugin>
```

---

[4]"XML." http://en.wikipedia.org/wiki/XML.

Of course, you can choose any format for the manifest file, like JSON or a custom text format. The important thing is that the plug-in's DLL does not contain any information about the plug-in or its commands. Only the manifest file holds that information.

Plug-ins can be located in a directory structure, as shown in Listing 11-5.

Listing 11-5. Example of Plug-in and Editor Directory Structure

```
\Plugins
    \Example1
        Example1.dll
        Example1.plugin.xml
    \Example2
        Example2.dll
        Example2.plugin.xml

EditorCore.dll (the editor code library)
EditorUI.exe (the main editor application)
```

One reason for storing the plug-in information inside external files is that plug-ins can be listed (with all their details) in the editor's plug-in manager without being loaded into memory. In this way, you can avoid loading some plug-ins you do not need to load, but still have information about them. For example, there can be special editor configurations for lighting artists, programmers, or level designers, and these configuration files can be shared among users.

As you can see from the plug-in manifest, you have added information about the name, description, author, and other useful properties, but also about the plug-in's dependencies (other plug-in GUIDs[5]). Optionally, there should be information about the commands, such as name, description, parameters, and return values, since you do not store this information in the C++ source files. This information can be used by a debug layer to check the command syntax at runtime and help the discovery of incorrect command calls during development.

For plug-in identification, you will use a GUID in the form shown in Listing 11-6.

Listing 11-6. The GUID Structure Used to Identify Plug-ins

```
// A plug-in unique ID, in a GUID form (see more about Microsoft
// GUID) and online/offline GUID generators
struct PluginGuid
{
    PluginGuid();

    // construct the guid from several elements/parts
    // example:
    // as text: 31D9B906-6125-4784-81FF-119C15267FCA
    // as C++: 0x31d9b906, 0x6125, 0x4784, 0x81,
    // 0xff, 0x11, 0x9c, 0x15, 0x26, 0x7f, 0xca
    PluginGuid(uint32 a, uint16 b, uint16 c, uint8 d,
 uint8 e, uint8 f, uint8 g, uint8 h, uint8 i,
        uint8 j, uint8 k);

    bool operator == (const PluginGuid& rOther) const;

    // convert a GUID string to binary
    // string format: "11191906-6125-4784-81FF-119C15267FC3"
    bool fromString(const char* pGUID);
```

---

[5]Wikipedia. "Globally unique identifier." http://en.wikipedia.org/wiki/Globally_unique_identifier.

```
    uint32 data1;
    uint16 data2;
    uint16 data3;
    uint8 data4[8];
};
```

You will use the interface shown in Listing 11-7 to get information about the discovered plug-ins (gathered from the plug-in manifest files).

Listing 11-7. The Interface that Describes a Plug-in (from the Plug-in Manifest)

```
struct IPluginInfo
{
    virtual ~IPluginInfo(){}
    virtual const char* GetName() const = 0;
    virtual const char* GetDescription() const = 0;
    virtual const char* GetAuthor() const = 0;
    virtual const char* GetWebsiteUrl() const = 0;
    virtual PluginGuid GetGuid() const = 0;
    virtual Version GetVersion() const = 0;
    virtual Version GetMinEditorVersion() const = 0;
    virtual Version GetMaxEditorVersion() const = 0;
    virtual const char* GetIconFilename() const = 0;
    virtual bool IsUnloadable() const = 0;
    virtual PluginGuidArray GetPluginDependencies()
                                    const = 0;
};
```

The plug-in interface methods are easy to understand, but let's talk about GetMinEditorVersion() and GetMaxEditorVersion(). These methods are used to check whether the plug-in can be loaded into the current editor and help avoid loading plug-ins that are not supposed to run under newer or older editor versions.

The simple creation process of new plug-ins and commands should be the crux of this system, thus coding new command sets hosted in the plug-ins should be straightforward. In the editor core API, there is an interface each plug-in must implement on its side, called IPlugin, as shown in Listing 11-8.

Listing 11-8. The Interface to be Implemented by a Plug-in

```
struct IPlugin
{
    virtual ~IPlugin(){}
    virtual void Initialize(IEditor* pEditor) = 0;
    virtual void Shutdown() = 0;
    virtual bool IsCommandEnabled(TPfnCommand pCmdFunc)= 0;
};
```

Commands

You will create the editor core as a C++ DLL. This handles the loading of plug-ins that are exposing editing commands. The GUI will call the commands using only the core editor interfaces (see Figure 11-2).

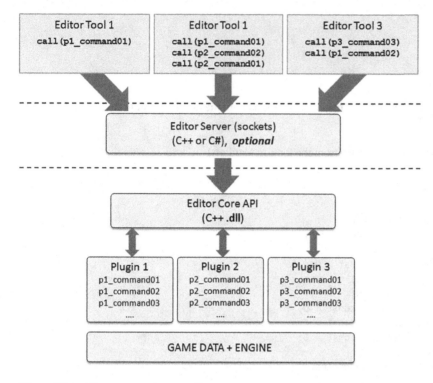

Figure 11-2. *The command system diagram*

The command system is designed as an RPC-like (remote procedure call) architecture, where commands are actually functions that are called with arguments and return one or more values. The call itself can be made directly using the editor core C++ API or the UI editor application connecting sockets to an editor core server, transmitting the command call data and then receiving the returned values.

A command executes only non-GUI-related code so it will not deal with the GUI functions itself, only engine calls and game data. The GUI code will take care of visual representation for the user, and it will call the available commands.

The plug-ins will expose their set of commands, but they will have nothing to do with the GUI itself. You can create a separate plug-in system for the editor's GUI. This is where the true decoupling kicks in, the editor core plug-ins being just "buckets" of non-GUI-related commands with the editor GUI using those commands. There is no need for a 1:1 match between the UI functions and the commands. You only need to expose the basic/simple commands, which should be generic enough to be used by multiple UI tools in various situations.

Command Parameters

When calling the commands, you have the option to send parameters to them, and for this you need to define the parameter type, direction, and description. This information is read from the plug-in's manifest file, but it's optional since the calling of commands is accomplished through a parameter set that is aware of the data types at the moment of setting the values. In Listing 11-9, you declare the IParameter interface.

Listing 11-9. The Command Parameter Interface

```
struct IParameter
{
    enum EDataType
    {
        eDataType_Unknown,
        eDataType_Int8,
        eDataType_Int16,
        eDataType_Int32,
        eDataType_Int64,
        eDataType_Float,
        eDataType_Double,
        eDataType_Text,
        eDataType_Handle
    };
    enum EDirection
    {
        eDirection_Input,
        eDirection_Output,
        eDirection_InputOutput
    };
    virtual ~IParameter(){}
    virtual const char* GetName() const = 0;
    virtual const char* GetDescription() const = 0;
    virtual EDataType GetDataType() const = 0;
    virtual EDirection GetDirection() const = 0;
    virtual bool IsArray() const = 0;
};
```

The IParameter interface is implemented by the editor core DLL, so plug-in developers do not need to care about the implementation, only what methods it provides, such as the name of the parameter, description, type, direction (if it's an in/out parameter), and whether the parameter is an array of the type specified.

To keep the parameter information in one place, you declare an IParameterDefinitions interface, which holds the parameter information list for a command, as seen in Listing 11-10.

Listing 11-10. The Parameter Definitions Container Interface

```
struct IParameterDefinitions
{
    virtual size_t GetCount() const = 0;
    virtual IParameter* Get(size_t aIndex) const = 0;
    virtual bool Add(
            const char* pName,
            IParameter::EDataType aDataType,
            const char* pDescription,
            IParameter::EDirection aDirection,
            bool bArray) = 0;
};
```

When calling the commands, you need to pass the parameters. For this, you will use a `IParameterValues` values "bag," which can set/get parameters and store the values. You can use other approaches for passing parameters, like `#define` extravaganza or templates to declare several command call forms with from one to ten parameters in their declaration. Listing 11-11 shows the parameter values interface.

Listing 11-11. The Parameter Values Container Interface

```
// Parameter values container, used to pass and receive
// in/out parameter values from a command call
struct IParameterValues
{
    virtual ~IParameterValues(){}
    virtual void SetInt8(const char* pParamName,
                         int8 aValue) = 0;
    virtual void SetInt16(const char* pParamName,
                          int16 aValue) = 0;
    virtual void SetInt32(const char* pParamName,
                          int32 aValue) = 0;
    virtual void SetInt64(const char* pParamName,
                          int64 aValue) = 0;
    virtual void SetFloat(const char* pParamName,
                          float aValue) = 0;
    virtual void SetDouble(const char* pParamName,
                           double aValue) = 0;
    virtual void SetText(const char* pParamName,
                         const char* pValue) = 0;
    virtual void SetHandle(const char* pParamName,
                           Handle aValue) = 0;

    virtual void SetInt8Array(const char* pParamName,
                              Int8Array aArray) = 0;
    virtual void SetInt16Array(const char* pParamName,
                               Int16Array aArray) = 0;
    virtual void SetInt32Array(const char* pParamName,
                               Int32Array aArray) = 0;
    virtual void SetInt64Array(const char* pParamName,
                               Int64Array aArray) = 0;
    virtual void SetFloatArray(const char* pParamName,
                               FloatArray aArray) = 0;
    virtual void SetDoubleArray(const char* pParamName,
                                DoubleArray aArray) = 0;
    virtual void SetTextArray(const char* pParamName,
                              TextArray aArray) = 0;
    virtual void SetHandleArray(const char* pParamName,
                                HandleArray aArray) = 0;

    virtual int8 GetInt8(
                    const char* pParamName) const = 0;
    virtual int16 GetInt16(
                    const char* pParamName) const = 0;
    virtual int32 GetInt32(
                    const char* pParamName) const = 0;
```

```
    virtual int64 GetInt64(
                    const char* pParamName) const = 0;
    virtual float GetFloat(
                    const char* pParamName) const = 0;
    virtual double GetDouble(
                    const char* pParamName) const = 0;
    virtual const char* GetText(
                    const char* pParamName) const = 0;
    virtual Handle GetHandle(
                    const char* pParamName) const = 0;

    virtual Int8Array GetInt8Array(
                    const char* pParamName) const = 0;
    virtual Int16Array GetInt16Array(
                    const char* pParamName) const = 0;
    virtual Int32Array GetInt32Array(
                    const char* pParamName) const = 0;
    virtual Int64Array GetInt64Array(
                    const char* pParamName) const = 0;
    virtual FloatArray GetFloatArray(
                    const char* pParamName) const = 0;
    virtual DoubleArray GetDoubleArray(
                    const char* pParamName) const = 0;
    virtual TextArray GetTextArray(
                    const char* pParamName) const = 0;
    virtual HandleArray GetHandleArray(
                    const char* pParamName) const = 0;

    // delete all parameter values
    virtual void Clear() = 0;
    // get the number of parameters this list holds
    virtual size_t GetCount() const = 0;
    // get the data type of parameter at given index
    virtual IParameter::EDataType GetDataType(
                    size_t aIndex) const = 0;
    // get the direction of parameter at given index
    virtual IParameter::EDirection GetDirection(
                    size_t aIndex) const = 0;
    // get the data type of parameter at given index
    virtual const char* GetName(size_t aIndex) const = 0;
    // is this parameter an array at given index?
    virtual bool IsArray(size_t aIndex) const = 0;
};
```

To avoid memory fragmentation due to frequent command calls, you would ideally manage the parameter values through a memory pool. The actual command is a callback function receiving a parameter values set, and is declared as shown in Listing 11-12.

Listing 11-12. The Command Callback Function Type

```
typedef void (*TPfnCommand)(IParameterValues* pParams);
```

For debugging and auto-documentation purposes, the editor core API can provide detailed command information through the ICommand interface, which can hold the command description from the plug-in manifest file, plus the command callback function pointer, as shown in Listing 11-13.

Listing 11-13. The Command Information Provider Interface

```
struct ICommand
{
    virtual ~ICommand(){}
    virtual const char* GetName() const = 0;
    virtual const char* GetDescription() const = 0;
    virtual const char* GetIconFilename() const = 0;
    virtual TPfnCommand GetCommandFunc() = 0;
    virtual const IParameterDefinitions*
                    GetParameterDefinitions() const = 0;
};
```

Direct Editor API Command Calls

You can call the editor core interface for executing commands directly from C++ or use a wrapper tool for another language like C# (SWIG). To call the commands in C++, use the code shown in Listing 11-14.

Listing 11-14. How to Call a Command

```
// create a parameter values bag
IParameterValues* pParams =
                    pEditor->CreateParameterValues();
// set some parameter values
pParams->SetInt32("someParam1", 123);
pParams->SetText("someName", "Elena Lenutza Nedelcu");
pParams->SetText("someOtherName", "Dorinel Nedelcu");
// the actual command call
pEditor->Call("someCommandName", pParams);
// retrieve the return values
float fRetVal = pParams->GetFloat("returnSomeValue");
int someNum = pParams->GetInt32("otherValue");
```

Remote Editor API Command Calls

You can use sockets for calling the commands remotely, since they're cross-platform and relatively easy to use from any language or environment. On the editor core DLL side, you will have a network server executable, and on the editor UI side, you will have a network client sending and receiving command data.

Communication can be accomplished through reliable UDP or TCP. For a local editor on the same machine, TCP would be okay even for LAN scenarios. If you are not so keen on using TCP because you consider it slow, UDP should suffice to send commands. All logic remains the same in this networked scenario, but this setup opens doors to online collaboration of multiple clients operating on the same data on the server. I'm not going to discuss this here, since it's a subject for a whole chapter (a challenging and interesting one!).

Networked editing is also feasible for debugging and remote in-editor live tutorials.

Putting It All Together

The editor can be implemented in Qt (just an example, chosen for its cross-platform support, though C# can also be supported using Mono on platforms other than Windows). This editor will be an empty skeleton that contains a plug-in manager dialog and nothing else, since all the functionality will be brought in by the plug-ins. Once again you need to emphasize the separation of the plug-in systems. They are two systems, one for the UI, and one for the editor core commands. UI plug-ins will use the commands found in the editor core plug-ins (see Figure 11-1 at the beginning of this chapter). The main UI editor can even do without a plug-in system if it's so intended, but the editor core command plug-ins will still exist.

Implementing a Plug-in with Commands

To ensure that you have a simple way of implementing new commands, the method of declaring commands and plug-ins must be straightforward. In the editor core API, IPlugin is the interface a plug-in must implement. To help rapid plug-in development, you can write a series of macros. In this sample plug-in, implementing a few commands would look like the code shown in Listing 11-15.

Listing 11-15. A Sample Plug-in Implementation

```
#include "EditorApi.h"

void example_my_command1(IParameterValues* pParams)
{
   // get our calling parameter values
    int numberOfHorses =
             pParams->GetInt32("numberOfHorses");
   std::string dailyMessage =
             pParams->GetText("dailyMessage");
   // do something important here for the command...

   // return some parameter values
   pParams->SetDouble("weightOfAllHorses", 1234.0f);
   pParams->SetText("userFullName", "Mihaela Claudia V.");
}

void example_my_command2(IParameterValues* pParams)
{
   // now here we'll try to grab an array
   FloatArray magicFloats =
               pParams->GetFloatArray("magicFloats");

   for (size_t i = 0; i < magicFloats.count; ++i)
   {
      float oneMagicFloat = magicFloats.elements[i];
      // do something majestic with the float...
   }
   // we do not need to return any value now
}

BEGIN_PLUGIN
```

```
void Initialize(IEditor* pEditor)
{
    REGISTER_COMMAND(example_my_command1);
    REGISTER_COMMAND(example_my_command2);
}

// used to check if a command is disabled at that time
// can be helpful for UI to disable buttons in toolbars
// or other related visual feedback
bool IsCommandEnabled(TPfnCommand pCmdFunc)
{
    return true;
}

void Shutdown()
{
}

END_PLUGIN
```

Note that BEGIN_PLUGIN and END_PLUGIN are macros hiding the start/end of the IPlugin interface implementation. The Initialize method is called when the plug-in is loaded into the editor. You are also registering the plug-in's commands by just referring invoking the global functions example_my_command1 and example_my_command1. The Shutdown method is called when the plug-in is unloaded (no need to call the unregister commands; this can be tracked and executed by the editor core itself, since it knows the IPlugin pointer when the commands are registered). The IsCommandEnabled method is used to verify whether a command has the status of "enabled" so it can be called/executed.

Be sure to name the commands in a way that avoids conflicts. Usually some sort of group naming, like the name of the plug-in and the actual command action name, should be enough, like assets_reload, assets_set_tag, assets_delete, or if you prefer camel-case style, Assets_SetTag.

The generated plug-in will be named example.dll and will be accompanied by its manifest file, example.plugin.xml. Of course, the plug-in must export a CreatePluginInstance global function so the editor core can load it and instantiate the IPlugin implementation.

Events

To make the plug-ins aware of events occurring in the editor ecosystem, they can register themselves as event sinks, as shown in Listing 11-16.

Listing 11-16. An Event Sink, Which Can Be Implemented by the Plug-ins

```
// Every plug-in can register its event sink so it can
// receive notifications about events happening in the
// editor ecosystem, coming from other plug-ins or the
// editor core itself
struct IEventSink
{
    // When the event sink call is received, before, during or
    // after the event was consumed
    // The eTriggerContext_During can be used to have
    // lengthy events being processed and many triggered to
```

```
    // update some progress bars
    enum ETriggerContext
    {
        eTriggerContext_Before,
        eTriggerContext_During,
        eTriggerContext_After
    };
    virtual ~IEventSink(){}
    virtual void OnEvent(IEvent* pEvent,
                         ETriggerContext aContext,
                         void* pUserData) = 0;
};
```

The IEventSink::OnEvent method is called whenever an event is triggered by other plug-ins or their commands and broadcast to the registered event sinks. The method receives a pointer to the triggered event interface (see Listing 11-17).

Listing 11-17. An Event, Implemented by the Trigger Code

```
// An event is triggered when certain actions are happening
// in the editor or its plug-ins. For example we can have an
// event at Save level or an object moved with the mouse
struct IEvent
{
    virtual ~IEvent(){}
    virtual const char* GetName() = 0;
    virtual void OnTrigger(void* pUserData) = 0;
    virtual void* GetUserData() = 0;
};
```

Listing 11-18 shows how to trigger an event.

Listing 11-18. Creating, Registering, and Triggering an Event

```
// we declare an event
struct MyEvent: IEvent
{
    virtual const char* GetName()
    {
        return "MyCoolEvent";
    }
    // this will be called when the event is triggered,
    // before being broadcast to all the event sinks
    // so the event can even modify the user data
    virtual void OnTrigger(void* pUserData)
    {
        // modify or store the pUserData
        m_pData = pUserData;
    }
    virtual void* GetUserData()
    {
        return m_pData;
    }
```

```
    uint8 m_pData;
} s_myEvent;

// we register an event (usually in the Initialize method
// of the plug-in)
...
REGISTER_EVENT(&s_myEvent);
...
// in some command, we trigger the event
void my_command(IParameterValues* pParams)
{
    uint8* pSomeData;
    // ....... do things with pSomeData
    g_pEditor->TriggerEvent(
                    &s_myEvent,
                    IEventSink::eTriggerContext_After,
                    pSomeData);
}
```

In some plug-ins, an event sink registered for a particular event would be notified of the event being triggered, as shown in Listing 11-19.

Listing 11-19. Creating and Registering an Event Sink

```
// declare our event sink
struct MyEventSink: IEventSink
{
    void OnEvent(IEvent* pEvent,
                    ETriggerContext aContext,
                    void* pUserData)
    {
        // is this the event we're looking for?
        if (!strcmp(pEvent->GetName(), "MyCoolEvent"))
        {
            uint8* pEventData = pEvent->GetUserData();
            // ...do things when that event was triggered
        }
    }
} s_myEventSink;

// inside the plug-in's Initialize method, register
// the event sink
...
pEditor->RegisterEventSink(&s_myEventSink);
...
```

In Figure 11-3, you can see a demo application of this system, with the editor skeleton having just one menu item and a settings dialog where plug-ins are managed.

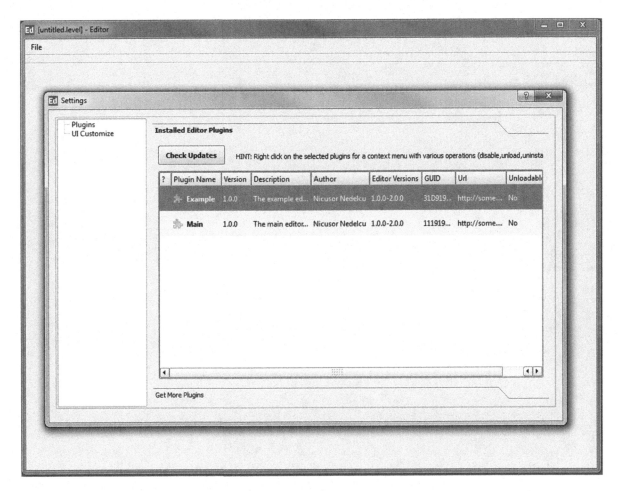

Figure 11-3. Skeleton editor UI application and settings dialog, with the plug-in manager (made with Qt)

Conclusion

Decoupling the UI from core editing functionality helps the development and fast feature-set iteration of game creation tools, since fewer hard-coded dependencies and monolithic schemes are used. The tools can be extended and used for a wide range of projects, the editor itself being quite agnostic to the game type and even the engine used. The solution presented here can be implemented in many ways, from the command system interfaces to the UI or plug-in system. In all cases, one thing remains constant: the use of UI-independent editing operations is separated from the tools' GUI using the command layer. I hope this article inspires you to make the right choices when creating extensible, elegant solutions for your game development tools.

CHAPTER 12

■ ■ ■

Building A Game Prototyping Tool for Android Mobile Devices

Gustavo Samour

You never truly know where inspiration will come from, or when it will happen. A game developer can be caught off guard at home, on the subway, or while on vacation. Forgetting an idea because one was not able to write it down can be a frustrating feeling. And, while finding a pen and paper is easy, oftentimes these tools are not robust enough to fully capture the essence of an idea. Sometimes something more sophisticated, like a game prototyping tool, is necessary to test and better express a concept. If a picture is worth a thousand words, then an interactive demo is worth a million.

We are used to seeing these tools on personal computers such as workstations and laptops. If inspiration strikes while at home or in the office, developers can boot up their machines and get to work. But if inspiration strikes while on the move, there's a good chance a long time will pass before having access to a computer. Fortunately, smartphones and tablets are powerful enough to run a game prototyping tool, and they are practical enough to allow us to use such a tool while we are out and about.

This chapter will show you how to write your own mobile game prototyping tool using AngelScript[1]. The first section provides basic information on how to set up your PC for Android programming. Those well versed in Android development, however, may want to skip the section on getting ready. The meat of this article is the script engine implementation in native code, and its integration with Java via the Java Native Interface. JNI is a standard programming interface for writing Java native methods[2].

Getting Ready for Development

This first section explains the purpose of this chapter and provides a description of the software to be written. There is also a message on scope, as there is more to the subject than can be covered in these pages. A list of required tools is shown, with a description of each one. And finally, you will find a brief explanation of the code structure for the software.

---

[1]Andreas Jönsson. "Angelscript." Accessed November 12, 2011. www.angelcode.com/angelscript/.
[2]Oracle Corporation. "JNI APIs and Developer Guides." Accessed April 9, 2014. http://docs.oracle.com/javase/8/docs/technotes/guides/jni/index.html.

A Game Prototyping Tool

For our purposes, a game prototyping tool is a specialized, limited version of a game authoring tool. Its goal is to allow the validation of a game idea; the program does not facilitate the creation of a full game. Some examples of complete authoring tools are UDK by Epic Games, Unity Engine by Unity Technologies, and GameMaker by YoYo Games. The tool you will develop in this chapter was envisioned with GameMaker in mind. I'll show a minor feature set in this chapter, and you can take it further in the direction that suits you best.

Scope

A prototyping tool is made up of many parts, among them a scripting engine, and an entire book can be written just about that. To keep both the text and the code short, some compromises have to be made. First of all, the reader is expected to possess knowledge of certain tools, programming languages, and APIs. Most concepts are not explained from the ground up. Second, since the focus is on functionality, the resulting application's user interface will be minimal and will allow for 2D prototypes. Third, optimization and best practices in coding are not a priority. Fourth, not every snippet of code is written out. Most notably, all Java import and C/C++ #include statements have been left out. However, the complete source code is included in the download pack on the book's page at www.apress.com. Finally, implementing features that are not essential to understanding the system are left as an exercise for the reader.

Even though our scope is limited, after finishing this chapter, you will have a powerful tool in your hands. You will be able to add and remove game objects in a scene, as well as give each scene object a script to follow at runtime. After the initial setup, a different screen will allow the scene to be played, paused, and stopped. During playback, game object scripts will control the action. Each object will be capable of modifying its own properties, a feature that should be sufficient for testing various styles of gameplay.

Purpose

This article was written to give the reader a low-level glimpse into the world of game creation tools in a mobile environment. While the subject is massive, I will boil it down to essentials by developing a tool of limited capability. Hopefully, the article will spark an interest and you will explore the subject matter further. It would be interesting to see the end result being improved with unique contributions.

Tools

It is not uncommon for game development tools to rely on other tools, and to build your Android application you'll need the help of the software listed in Table 12-1.

Table 12-1. *Tools Required to Create the Game Prototyping Tool (GPT)*

Software	Purpose
Android SDK	Java APIs for developing Android applications
Android NDK	C++ APIs for developing native Android libraries
Eclipse	IDE for building and debugging Android applications
ADT Plug-in	Allows Eclipse to work with Android applications
Cygwin	Unix-like environment that runs on MS Windows
AngelScript	Library for building and executing game object scripts

The Android SDK is a set of APIs for developing applications using the Java language. Because the SDK has been revised and different devices come with different versions of the Android operating system, there are different API levels. At the time of this writing, the most recent is API Level 19. It corresponds to version 4.4 of the OS, otherwise known as the Kit Kat release[3]. However, you can use a lower API Level to be able to target older devices. The user interface, which comprises the majority of code in your game prototyping tool, will be written in Java.

As a way to allow native development on the Android platform and for developers to take advantage of existing C/C++ code libraries, the NDK was released. Like the SDK, it has been through several revisions, and the latest one at the time of writing is Revision 9d[4]. The core of your tool, the scripting system, will be written in C/C++ and compiled into a shared library.

To make development easier, an integrated development environment (IDE) will be used for writing code and building the project. Developers nowadays have their choice of software, and the reader is welcome to use their preferred IDE. However, it is worth mentioning that Eclipse makes it easy to write Android applications. The ADT plug-in adds project templates for Android development, tools to create user interface layouts, Android debugging capabilities, and more.[5]

Cygwin is an optional tool that provides a Unix-like environment on the Windows platform[6]. You will use it for building native code into libraries usable by Android applications. The Android NDK comes with the `ndk-build` shell script that must run in a Unix-like environment. The reason it's optional is that as of NDK Revision 7, there is a new Windows-compatible build script. The `ndk-build.cmd` script allows developers to build native code libraries on a Windows system without Cygwin. However, the documentation lists this script as an experimental feature of NDK Revision 7, so it may have issues.

The scripting library used in this article is AngelScript. This is an open source project developed by Andreas Jönsson that includes contributions by many other developers. You will use it to build the core of your game prototyping tool, which is a script engine. It will be responsible for initializing and updating a scene full of game objects.

Code Structure

An Android application is generally written in Java and is made up of one or more Activity classes. Each activity can set one or more View objects as a user interface. One activity is enough for the prototyping tool, which will implement three different views: a scene editing canvas, a script text editor, and a scene-playing screen. A list of game objects will be kept when editing a scene and when playing it, so you'll write a couple of classes that represent game objects. To run scripts while playing a scene, the tool will interface with a basic scripting engine written in C/C++. Java code will take care of calling native code and getting what it needs from the script engine; this will happen via the Java Native Interface. Some advantages of JNI are reusing an existing code library without converting it to another language, better performance by running some processes in a native environment instead of a virtual machine, and ease of porting to other platforms that support native code. On the C/C++ side there will be a main source file and a pair of .h/.cpp files for a script engine class. Table 12-2 lists all source files and their purpose.

---

[3]Google Inc. "Codenames, Tags, and Build Numbers." Accessed April 9, 2014. `http://source.android.com/source/build-numbers.html`.
[4]Google Inc. "Android NDK." Accessed November 12, 2011. `http://developer.android.com/tools/sdk/ndk/index.html`.
[5]Google Inc. "ADT Plug-in." Accessed November 12, 2011. `http://developer.android.com/tools/sdk/eclipse-adt.html`.
[6]Red Hat. "Cygwin." Accessed November 12, 2011. `www.cygwin.com/`.

Table 12-2. *GPT Source Files*

Filename	Purpose
GPTActivity.java	Fulfills the requirement of an Activity class
GPTEditorGameObject.java	GameObject class with properties related to the Scene Editor
GPTSceneEditorView.java	Custom View for placing objects in a scene
GPTScriptEditorView.java	Custom View for editing scripts manually
GPTJNILib.java	Exposes native functions to other Java classes
GPTGameObject.java	GameObject class with properties related to the Scene Player
GPTScenePlayerView.java	Custom View for playing a scene
GPTMain.cpp	Implements the native functions declared in GPTJNILib.java
GPTScriptEngine.h	Declaration of the script engine's class and members
GPTScriptEngine.cpp	Implementation of the script engine's member functions

User Interface Implementation

Now that the required tools are installed, let's create a new Android project. First, open the Eclipse IDE if it's not already running. The following dialogs may be different on other machines, but should still be fairly consistent. Click the File menu, go to New and click Project. In the New Project dialog box, select the Android Application Project wizard and click Next. Write down a project name, such as "GPT" or "Game Prototyping Tool." Next, change the package name to com.gametoolgems.gpt or something similar. Now, choose a build SDK and a minimum required SDK. The code I've written requires at least API Level 10, but with a few changes, it can compile on a lower SDK version. Select an SDK that is appropriate for the devices you want to target and click Next. Keep going until the wizard asks for an activity name and choose an appropriate name, like "GPTActivity." Keep going through the wizard until you can click the Finish button. A new Android project will be created in your workspace folder.

GPTActivity

The main activity class doesn't have to do much. In its onCreate method, it will make instances of the three View classes in the application and then bring the scene editor to the front. When handling the onBackPressed event, it will simply pass it forward to the current View. To do this, it needs to keep track of the current View so it will publicly expose a SetCurrentView method. Listing 12-1 represents the code for GPTActivity.

Listing 12-1. GPTActivity Class

```
public class GPTActivity extends Activity
{
  private View mCurrentView = null;
  public static GPTScriptEditorView scriptEditorView;
  public static GPTSceneEditorView sceneEditorView;
  public static GPTScenePlayerView scenePlayerView;

  @Override
  public void onCreate(Bundle savedInstanceState)

    {
    super.onCreate(savedInstanceState);
```

```java
    // Load native code library
    GPTJNILib.Load();

    // Create views and set current view to scene editor
    scriptEditorView = new GPTScriptEditorView(this);
    scenePlayerView = new GPTScenePlayerView(this);
    sceneEditorView = new GPTSceneEditorView(this);
    SetCurrentView(sceneEditorView);
  }

  public void SetCurrentView(View v)
  {
    mCurrentView = v;
    setContentView(v);
  }

  @Override
  public void onBackPressed()
  {
    if (mCurrentView == scriptEditorView)
      scriptEditorView.onBackPressed(this);
    else if (mCurrentView == sceneEditorView)
      sceneEditorView.onBackPressed(this);
    else if(mCurrentView == scenePlayerView)
      scenePlayerView.onBackPressed(this);
  }
}
```

GPTJNILib

Rather than give native member methods to each class that requires C/C++ interaction, the project will have an abstract class that exposes all the necessary native functions to the rest of the Java code. This simplifies JNI function naming on the C/C++ side. There are two main things the native code should do to interact with the scripting engine: set up a scene and update a scene. GPTJNILib.java only declares those two static functions, plus an additional function to load the C/C++ library itself, as shown in Listing 12-2.

Listing 12-2. GPTJNILib Abstract Class

```java
public abstract class GPTJNILib
{
  public static void Load()
  {
    System.loadLibrary("gptjni");
  }

  public static native void Initialize(
    GPTEditorGameObject[] gameObjects);

  public static native void Update(
    float deltaTime,
    ArrayList<GPTGameObject> updatedGameObjects);
}
```

Scene Editor and Script Editor

Generally, a game creation tool allows drawing or importing sprites, then generating prefabricated objects, or "prefabs," that use those sprites. Behavior-modifying scripts can also be added to the prefabs. When placed in a scene, those prefabs become unique game objects. For your simplified prototyping tool, colored circles take the place of objects and each object has exactly one script. The first step in creating a scene editor is to add a couple of classes that represent a game object, as shown in Listings 12-3 and 12-4.

Listing 12-3. GPTEditorGameObject Class

```
public class GPTEditorGameObject
{
  private static int NEXT_ID = 0;
  public static final int DEFAULT_COLOR = Color.WHITE;
  private static final String DEFAULT_SCRIPT =
  ""                                               + "\n" +
  "void OnUpdate(float deltaTime)"                 + "\n" +
  "{"                                              + "\n" +
  "  "                                             + "\n" +
  "}"                                              + "\n" +
  ""                                               + "\n" +
                                                     "\n";

  public int id;
  public float x;
  public float y;
  public int color;
  public String script = DEFAULT_SCRIPT;

  GPTEditorGameObject(float objX, float objY, int objColor)
  {
    id = NEXT_ID++; // assign unique ID to game object
    x = objX;
    y = objY;
    color = objColor;
  }
}
```

Listing 12-4. GPTGameObject Class

```
public class GPTGameObject
{
  public int id;
  public float x;
  public float y;
  public int color;

  GPTGameObject
    (int objId, float objX, float objY, int objColor)
  {
    id = objId;
    x = objX;
    y = objY;
    color = objColor;
  }
}
```

As you can see, all the class does is store five properties for an object: an identifier, position along the X axis, position along the Y axis, a color, and a script to run when playing the scene. The difference between the editor and player versions of the class is that the editor sets an identifier automatically, and the player doesn't need to store the script code. The second step in creating a scene editor is adding a View class, which you'll call GPTSceneEditorView. Aside from creating a formal design document, the best way to explain what the code will do is to look at a screenshot of the result, such as Figure 12-1.

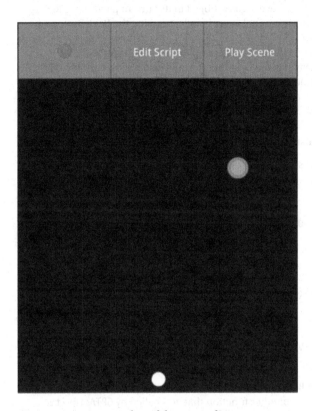

Figure 12-1. *A screenshot of the scene editor*

Figure 12-1 shows the finished scene editor. The user interface has three buttons and an empty area that represents the scene. The GUI button on the left shows the current color; every time a new object is added, its color is set to the current color. Tapping on this button cycles between different colors. The middle button is for editing the selected object's script. It brings up the GPTScriptEditorView. When users are done editing the scene, the button on the right takes them to the scene player screen. Tapping inside the empty area adds a new object. If the tap is on top of an existing object, it becomes the selected object. Selection is visually represented with a gray outline. Dragging works as one would expect it to: the selected object is moved to the desired location.

Because the main focus of this chapter is the scripting engine, code for the GPTSceneEditorView and GPTScriptEditorView classes has been omitted from these pages. As an exercise, feel free to implement those classes in a custom way. But if you prefer the original code, it can be downloaded from www.apress.com.

Scene Player

The scene player is where the game prototype comes to life. This is the screen where the objects' scripts run and all the action takes place. The user interface is presented in a similar fashion to that of the scene editor: an empty area represents the scene, and the GUI area consists of a play/pause button and a stop button. Pressing the play button runs the GPTJNILib class's native Update function in a loop and swaps the button with a pause button. Pressing the Pause button causes the application to skip updates, which keeps every game object in its current position. The Stop button resets the scene, bringing all the game objects back to their initial state. Finally, pressing the Back button on the device closes the scene player and shows the scene editor.

The first thing you need for playing is a list of game objects that will be kept up to date. Then you'll need a variable to tell if the simulation is playing, as opposed to being paused or stopped. You'll also need a variable that holds the last frame's timestamp, which is used to compute delta time. The last two member variables in the class, OBJECT_RADIUS and GUI_SCREEN_HEIGHT_PCT, determine the size of each game object and the height of the simulation control buttons, respectively. See Listing 12-5 for the code.

Listing 12-5. GPTScenePlayerView Member Variables, Constructor, and Example of OnBackPressed Function

```
private ArrayList<GPTGameObject> mUpdatedGameObjects;
private boolean mIsPlaying;
private long mLastTime;
private static final float OBJECT_RADIUS = 20.0f;
private static final float GUI_SCREEN_HEIGHT_PCT = 0.125f;

public GPTScenePlayerView(Context context) {
  super(context);
  mIsPlaying = false;
  mUpdatedGameObjects = newArrayList<GPTGameObject>();
}

  public void onBackPressed(GPTActivity activity) {
    activity.SetCurrentView(GPTActivity.sceneEditorView);
  }
```

There is nothing special about the constructor or the OnBackPressed function. The first just calls the base constructor and sets some default values, while the second is a handler function that gets called by GPTActivity whenever the user presses the back key on their device. In this particular case, pressing this key on the scene player takes the user back to the scene editor.

SetSceneObjects is the first major function of the scene player class. It takes a list of GPTEditorGameObject instances and populates an internal list of GPTGameObject instances, losing the String-typed script property in the process. It also turns the list of editor objects into an array and passes the array to native code via GPTJNILib's Initialize function as shown in Listing 12-6.

Listing 12-6. GPTScenePlayerView SetSceneObjects Function

```
public void SetSceneObjects(
ArrayList<GPTEditorGameObject> sceneObjects)
{
  mUpdatedGameObjects.clear();

  for (GPTEditorGameObject obj : sceneObjects)
{
    mUpdatedGameObjects.add(new GPTGameObject(
    obj.id, obj.x, obj.y, obj.color));
}
```

```
  GPTEditorGameObject[] gameObjects =
new GPTEditorGameObject[mUpdatedGameObjects.size()];

  GPTJNILib.Initialize(sceneObjects.toArray(gameObjects));
}
```

These two functions are fairly straightforward; if the user touches the GUI, the HandleGUITouch function is called, as shown in Listing 12-7.

Listing 12-7. GPTScenePlayerView Touch Functions

```
@Override
public boolean onTouchEvent(MotionEvent event) {

  PointerCoords coords = new PointerCoords();
  event.getPointerCoords(0, coords);

    if(event.getAction() == MotionEvent.ACTION_DOWN)
      HandleTouchDownEvent(coords.x, coords.y);

    return true;
}

private void HandleTouchDownEvent(float x, float y) {

  // If we touched the GUI, interact with it
  Rect guiRect = new Rect(0, 0, getWidth(),
    (int)((getHeight() * GUI_SCREEN_HEIGHT_PCT)));

  if (guiRect.contains((int)x, (int)y))
    HandleGUITouch(x, y);
}
```

If the user presses the play button, the mIsPlaying flag gets set to true, the timer is started, and the scene player's Update function will continually request an up-to-date list of game objects. If the Pause button is pressed, mIsPlaying is set to false. If the Stop button is pressed, the scene is reset directly; all game objects move back to their original positions as shown in Listing 12-8. The Update function is shown in Listing 12-9.

Listing 12-8. GPTScenePlayerView HandleGUITouch Function

```
private void HandleGUITouch(float x, float y) {

  Rect playPauseButtonRect =
    new Rect(0, 0, getWidth() / 2,
    (int)((getHeight() * GUI_SCREEN_HEIGHT_PCT)));

  Rect stopButtonRect =
    new Rect(getWidth() / 2, 0, getWidth(),
    (int)((getHeight() * GUI_SCREEN_HEIGHT_PCT)));

  if (playPauseButtonRect.contains((int)x, (int)y))
  {
    mIsPlaying = !mIsPlaying;
```

```
    // start timing
    if (mIsPlaying)
      mLastTime = System.nanoTime();
  }
  else if (stopButtonRect.contains((int)x, (int)y))
  {
    // reset game objects
    mIsPlaying = false;
    SetSceneObjects(
      GPTActivity.sceneEditorView.
          GetSceneObjects());
  }
}
```

Listing 12-9. GPTScenePlayerView Update Function

```
public void Update()
{
  if (mIsPlaying)
  {
    // Get updated game objects
    long currTime = System.nanoTime();
    float dt = (currTime - mLastTime) / 1000000000.0f;
    mLastTime = currTime;

    mUpdatedGameObjects.clear();
    GPTJNILib.Update(dt, mUpdatedGameObjects);
  }
}
```

Drawing the scene happens via Java's onDraw function. The desired behavior is for drawing to happen over and over again in a loop. But by default, the function is only called once. The way to get around that is by invalidating the draw region at the end of onDraw, which will force another call to the function. By forcing execution on every function call, you guarantee the desired loop. Pausing will set mIsPlaying to false, which will skip the body of the Update function. Stopping will do the same, but will additionally cause the state of the scene to be reset. Now let's look at the onDraw function as shown in Listing 12-10.

Listing 12-10. GPTScenePlayerView onDraw Function

```
@Override
protected void onDraw(Canvas c)
{
  // update scene first, then draw
  Update();

  super.onDraw(c);

  // Draw background
  Paint paint = new Paint();
  paint.setAntiAlias(true);
  paint.setColor(Color.BLACK);
  c.drawPaint(paint);
```

```
    // draw game objects
    for (int i = 0; i < mUpdatedGameObjects.size(); ++i)
    {
      GPTGameObject obj = mUpdatedGameObjects.get(i);

      paint.setColor(obj.color);
      c.drawCircle(obj.x, obj.y, OBJECT_RADIUS, paint);
    }

    // Draw UI
    paint.setColor(Color.GRAY);
    Rect rect = new Rect(0, 0, getWidth(),
      (int)(getHeight() * GUI_SCREEN_HEIGHT_PCT));

c.drawRect(rect, paint);

    String playPauseString = mIsPlaying ? "Pause" : "Play";
    Rect strBounds = new Rect();
    paint.setColor(Color.WHITE);
    paint.setTextSize(30);
    paint.setTextAlign(Align.CENTER);
    paint.getTextBounds(playPauseString, 0,
      playPauseString.length(), strBounds);
    c.drawText(playPauseString, getWidth() / 4,
      ((getHeight() * GUI_SCREEN_HEIGHT_PCT) +
      (strBounds.bottom - strBounds.top)) / 2, paint);
    paint.setColor(Color.BLACK);
    c.drawLine(getWidth() / 2, 0, getWidth() / 2,
      (getHeight() * GUI_SCREEN_HEIGHT_PCT), paint);

    String stopStr = "Stop";
    strBounds = new Rect();
    paint.setColor(Color.WHITE);
    paint.setTextSize(30);
    paint.setTextAlign(Align.CENTER);
    paint.getTextBounds(stopStr,0,stopStr.length(),strBounds);
    c.drawText(stopStr, getWidth() - (getWidth() / 4),
      ((getHeight() * GUI_SCREEN_HEIGHT_PCT) +
      (strBounds.bottom - strBounds.top)) / 2, paint);

    // Force re-draw
postInvalidate();
}
```

The first thing that happens, even before drawing, is updating the game objects with results from the script engine. Then, along with the GUI elements, all the objects are drawn. Finally, the postInvalidate function call makes sure onDraw is called again.

Good news: this function marks the last of the Java code! You are now ready to move on to native C/C++ with the scripting engine implementation.

Native Script Engine Implementation

In the last section, you declared two native functions in the GPTJNILib class, Initialize and Update. Their implementations are still missing, so you will take care of that in this section. What does it mean to initialize the script engine? It means setting up the scene as it was created in the editor, but now in the context of scripted objects. How about updating? So many different things can be thought of as taking part in updating a scene. For example, collision detection and input handling may be a part of updating. Creating and destroying objects can also be considered updating. But for your purposes, updating a scene means calling the OnUpdate script function on every game object. Detecting collisions, handling touch input, and creating and destroying objects are left as an exercise to the reader.

Building GPT's Native Library with Android NDK

Preparing the build setup for native code can be tricky at first, but once it works, it's highly unlikely that it will require changes. The first thing to do is build AngelScript for Android as a static library. There are many ways to set up for building, but the following is an easy way.

1. Inside the AngelScript source distribution, there is a /projects/android folder. Navigate to it, and create a subfolder named jni.

2. Move the Android.mk file from /projects/android to the new /projects/android/jni folder.

3. Open the Android.mk file and make the following changes:

- Replace the line

```
LOCAL_PATH:= $(call my-dir)/../../source
```

with

```
LOCAL_PATH:= $(call my-dir)/../../../source
```

- Add the following lines at the end of the file:

```
include $(CLEAR_VARS)
LOCAL_MODULE := dummy
LOCAL_STATIC_LIBRARIES := libangelscript
include $(BUILD_SHARED_LIBRARY)
```

4. Open Cygwin, navigate to the android project's folder within AngelScript (i.e., /cygdrive/c/angelcode/angelscript/projects/android) and run the ndk-build script. For example, if the Android NDK was installed in C:\android-ndk-r9d, then the command would be

```
/cygdrive/c/android-ndk-r9d/ndk-build [ENTER]
```

Adding an extra ../ to Android.mk is required because in the previous step, that file was moved one folder deeper than it used to be. Adding the four lines at the end is necessary because a static library doesn't have to build on its own—unless other code depends on it. In this case, you are using a dummy library to create a dependency. After running ndk-build, you should have a libangelscript.a static library file.

The next step is to create a jni folder inside the game prototype tool's project folder. Copy the libangelscript.a file into the jni folder and create two files, Android.mk and Application.mk, inside that same folder.

The Android.mk file tells the build system which source files to compile, which libraries to link, and which type of library to output, as shown in Listing 12-11.

Listing 12-11. Android.mk File

```
LOCAL_PATH:= $(call my-dir)

# Declare the prebuilt AngelScript static library

include $(CLEAR_VARS)
LOCAL_MODULE    := libangelscript
LOCAL_SRC_FILES := libangelscript.a

include $(PREBUILT_STATIC_LIBRARY)

# Build our JNI shared library

include $(CLEAR_VARS)

LOCAL_MODULE    := libgptjni
LOCAL_CFLAGS    := -Werror
LOCAL_CPPFLAGS  := -fexceptions

LOCAL_SRC_FILES :=      GPTMain.cpp \
                       GPTScriptEngine.cpp

LOCAL_LDLIBS    := -llog
LOCAL_STATIC_LIBRARIES := libangelscript

include $(BUILD_SHARED_LIBRARY)
```

You will use containers from the Standard Template Library, or STL, in your native code. The Android NDK comes with its own version of STL and must be built. The Application.mk file has a single line that tells the NDK to build STL and to give us access to it (see Listing 12-12).

Listing 12-12. Application.mk File

```
APP_STL := gnustl_static
```

GPTScriptEngine

Let's briefly go over the requirements for the script engine. It should be able to take a scene as a collection of game objects, then create and manage a representation of that scene. The goal is to allow calling script functions on each object from within C/C++, which, along with compiling scripts, is the next requirement for the engine. The only script function you want to call in your simplified system is OnUpdate. But each object can implement it differently; this shows the power and flexibility of the prototyping tool. One last requirement is a way to reset the scene. The idea is to forget about the current collection of game objects and initialize the system with a new set of objects. An example is a situation in which the user navigates back to the editor, makes changes to the scene, and returns to the scene player.

The header file GPTScriptEngine.h is the blueprint for your scripting implementation, as shown in Listing 12-13.

Listing 12-13. GPTScriptEngine.h File

```
#ifndef _GPT_SCRIPT_ENGINE_H_
#define _GPT_SCRIPT_ENGINE_H_

#include "angelscript.h"
#include <vector>

struct ScriptModule
{
  int id;
  asIScriptModule* pModule;
};

struct GameObject
{
  int id;
  float x;
  float y;
  int color;
};

class GPTScriptEngine
{
public:

  GPTScriptEngine();
  ~GPTScriptEngine();

  bool AddGameObject(int id, float x, float y, int color,
    const char* scriptCode);

  void Update(float deltaTime);

  void GetUpdatedObjects(std::vector<GameObject>& objects);

  void Reset();

private:

  typedef std::vector<ScriptModule> ScriptModuleVector;

  asIScriptModule* BuildScriptModule(int gameObjectId, const
    char* scriptCode);

  asIScriptModule* FindScriptModule(int moduleId);

  asIScriptEngine* m_pScriptEngine;

  asIScriptContext* m_pScriptContext;

  std::vector<ScriptModule> m_scriptModules;
};
```

```
#endif  // _GPT_SCRIPT_ENGINE_H_
```

The ScriptModule structure maps a game object to an AngelScript module. Your basic implementation uses one module per game object, which is a very simple way to integrate scripting, however it imposes a big overhead for the application. A better way would be to use script classes, which are a standard part of AngelScript. For your purposes, one module for each game object is good enough.

Having a vector of ScriptModule instances helps iterate through all the game objects and call special script functions on them, such as Update. The GameObject structure is a helper that allows the script engine to provide an updated vector of objects via the GetUpdatedObjects function. The other important members are the AngelScript engine and context. Only one context is necessary for simple scripting.

Now that the blueprint is finished, let's begin with the GPTScriptEngine.cpp implementation file. You will define some common script code that will be added to all of your AngelScript modules. First, you need a scripted representation of a game object to be able to modify properties like position and color. Second, a global game object is created. Since this code will be added to every module, each instance will be global only to its unique module. The reason to make it global is to allow access to game object properties via a named reference (i.e., me.color). Finally, a set of global functions is defined. PreInit is called automatically when adding a game object to the system and it copies the property values to the scripted representation. GetProperties is called in a post-update step to gather the values of each game object and pass them along to the GUI. Listing 12-14 shows C/C++ code that defines strings with AngelScript code inside.

Listing 12-14. Common Script Code for All Modules

```
const char* classesCode =                                      \
"                                                        \n" \
"class CGameObject                                       \n" \
"{                                                       \n" \
"  public int   id;                                      \n" \
"  public float  x;                                      \n" \
"  public float  y;                                      \n" \
"  public int   color;                                   \n" \
"}                                                       \n" \
"                                                        \n" \
;

const char* globalObjectsCode =                                \
"CGameObject me;                                         \n" \
;

const char* globalFunctionsCode =                              \
"                                                        \n" \
"void PreInit(float x, float y, int color)              \n" \
"{                                                       \n" \
"  me.id     = id;                                       \n" \
"  me.x      = x;                                        \n" \
"  me.y      = y;                                        \n" \
"  me.color  = color;                                    \n" \
"}                                                       \n" \
"                                                        \n" \
"void GetProperties(float&out x,float&out y,int&out color) \n" \
"{                                                       \n" \
"  id         = me.x;                                    \n" \
"  x          = me.x;                                    \n" \
```

```
"   y          = me.y;                                            \n" \
"   color      = me.color;                                        \n" \
"}                                                                \n" \
"                                                                 \n" \
;
```

The lifecycle of the script system requires two things: an AngelScript engine and an AngelScript context, which you'll use for executing scripts. An optional but important step is to set a callback function that AngelScript uses for reporting errors, warnings, and other information. The current one just writes the message to the Android log. But a better system would pass the message to the GUI. Since the user should find out about script errors as soon as possible, a good idea would be to build the code in the script editor and inform of any errors then. Listing 12-15 shows the implementation of the script engine's constructor, destructor, and message callback functions.

Listing 12-15. Script Engine Constructor and Destructor

```
void MessageCallback(const asSMessageInfo *msg, void *param)
{
  const char* type = "UNKNOWN";
  if(msg->type == asMSGTYPE_ERROR)
    type = "ERROR";
  else if(msg->type == asMSGTYPE_WARNING)
    type = "WARNING";
  else if(msg->type == asMSGTYPE_INFORMATION)
    type = "INFO";

  LOGE("%s (%d, %d) : %s : %s\n",
    msg->section, msg->row, msg->col,
    type, msg->message);
}

GPTScriptEngine:: GPTScriptEngine()
{
  m_pScriptEngine=asCreateScriptEngine(ANGELSCRIPT_VERSION);
  m_pScriptContext = m_pScriptEngine->CreateContext();

  m_pScriptEngine->SetMessageCallback(
    asFUNCTION(MessageCallback), 0, asCALL_CDECL);
}

GPTScriptEngine::~GPTScriptEngine()
{
  m_pScriptContext->Release();
  m_pScriptContext = NULL;

  m_pScriptEngine->Release();
  m_pScriptEngine = NULL;
}
```

The next member function to be implemented is AddGameObject. This method receives all the properties of a game object and the script it should run. The function builds the script into a module and creates a new entry in the m_scriptModules vector. In order to give the scripted game object the same values as the native object, a call is made to the PreInit script function in the module. And now that the new object is in a container, the system keeps track of it and later calls the OnUpdate script function on it, as Listing 12-16 demonstrates.

Listing 12-16. AddGameObject and BuildScriptModule Functions

```cpp
bool GPTScriptEngine::AddGameObject(int id, float x, float y, int color, const char* scriptCode)
{
  // Build an AS module using the code
  asIScriptModule* pScriptModule =
    BuildScriptModule(id, scriptCode);

  if (pScriptModule)
  {
    // Call 'PreInit' on the script's game object
    asIScriptFunction* pPreInitFunction =
      pScriptModule->GetFunctionByDecl(
        "void PreInit(int id,float x,
        float y, int color)");

    m_pScriptContext->Prepare(pPreInitFunction);

    m_pScriptContext->SetArgDWord(0, id);
    m_pScriptContext->SetArgFloat(1, x);
    m_pScriptContext->SetArgFloat(2, y);
    m_pScriptContext->SetArgDWord(3, color);

    int retCode = m_pScriptContext->Execute();
    if(retCode != asEXECUTION_FINISHED)
    {
      // PreInit didn't finish executing.
      return false;
    }

    // Add module to list
    ScriptModule module;
    module.id = id;
    module.pModule = pScriptModule;
    m_scriptModules.push_back(module);

    return true;
  }
  else
  {
    // PreInit didn't compile. Do error handling.
  }
}

asIScriptModule* GPTScriptEngine::BuildScriptModule
(int id, const char* scriptCode)
{
  // Create a new script module
  std::stringstream moduleStream;
  moduleStream << id;
  std::string modName = moduleStream.str();
```

165

```
asIScriptModule *pScriptModule =
  m_pScriptEngine->GetModule(modName.c_str(),
    asGM_ALWAYS_CREATE);

// Load and add the script sections to the module
pScriptModule->AddScriptSection(
  "mainSection", scriptCode);

pScriptModule->AddScriptSection(
  "classesSection", classesCode);

pScriptModule->AddScriptSection(
  "globalObjectsSection", globalObjectsCode);

pScriptModule->AddScriptSection(
  "globalFunctionsSection", globalFunctionsCode);

// Build the module
int retCode = pScriptModule->Build();

if( retCode < 0 )
{
  // Build failed, delete the module and return NULL
  m_pScriptEngine->DiscardModule(modName.c_str());
  return NULL;
}

return pScriptModule;
}
```

The BuildScriptModule function creates an empty module, adds the object's source code, and also adds the common code you defined previously. It compiles the combined script and returns an AngelScript module if successful.

So far, the functions you've implemented don't make the game objects come to life; this will happen when you update the scripting system. Each object has a script function called OnUpdate that dictates its behavior at every step of the game loop. The scripting engine iterates through the collection of game objects and calls that function on each module, as shown in Listing 12-17.

Listing 12-17. The Script Engine's Update Function

```
void GPTScriptEngine::Update(float deltaTime)
{
  // Call the "OnUpdate" script function on every module
  for (size_t i = 0; i < m_scriptModules.size(); ++i)
  {
    asIScriptModule* pScriptModule =
      m_scriptModules[i].pModule;

    asIScriptFunction* pOnUpdateFunction =
      pScriptModule->GetFunctionByDecl(
        "void OnUpdate(float dt)"
        );
```

```
    m_pScriptContext->Prepare(pOnUpdateFunction);
    m_pScriptContext->SetArgFloat(0, deltaTime);
    int retCode = m_pScriptContext->Execute();
    if(retCode != asEXECUTION_FINISHED)
    {
      // OnUpdate didn't finish executing.
    }
  }
}
```

With the game objects now being updated every frame, their behavior is alive inside the script engine. However, you still can't visualize it. The Java-based user interface doesn't know what's happening in the script world just yet. One way to change that situation is to gather an updated collection of game objects from the script engine and send it via JNI. The GUI will then replace its current object collection with the updated one. As a first step, let's implement the GetUpdatedObjects member function, which builds a collection of game objects from the current state in the script engine, as shown in Listing 12-18.

Listing 12-18. The GetUpdatedObjects Function

```
void GPTScriptEngine::
GetUpdatedObjects(std::vector<GameObject>& updatedObjects)
{
  // For each script, call the GetProperties function
  for (size_t i = 0; i < m_scriptModules.size(); ++i)
  {
    asIScriptModule* pScriptModule =
      m_scriptModules[i].pModule;

    asIScriptFunction* pGetPropertiesFunction =
      pScriptModule->GetFunctionByDecl(
        "void GetPropertyValues(
          int&out id, float&out x,
          float&out y,
          int&out color)");

    m_pScriptContext->Prepare(pGetPropertiesFunction);

    GameObject obj;
    obj.id = m_scriptModules[i].id;

    m_pScriptContext->SetArgAddress(0, &obj.x);
    m_pScriptContext->SetArgAddress(1, &obj.y);
    m_pScriptContext->SetArgAddress(2, &obj.color);

    int retCode = m_pScriptContext->Execute();
    if(retCode != asEXECUTION_FINISHED)
    {
      // GetProperties didn't finish executing.
      continue;
    }

    updatedObjects.push_back(obj);
  }
}
```

You now have enough code to add objects to a scripted scene and update them. You also are halfway into sending the updated objects back to the Java GUI. But in its essence, scene playback is already possible. There's only one thing missing. What if the user, after watching a playback of the scene, decides to go back to the scene editor and delete an object? What if they want to add objects or edit the script of an existing object? The script system needs a way to reset itself to allow initialization of a new or modified scene. The Reset function removes all the script modules from the engine, as shown in Listing 12-19.

Listing 12-19. The Reset Function

```
void GPTScriptEngine::Reset()
{
  // Remove all modules from script engine
  for (size_t i = 0; i < m_scriptModules.size(); ++i)
  {
    std::stringstream moduleStream;
    moduleStream << m_scriptModules[i].id;
    std::string modName = moduleStream.str();
    m_pScriptEngine->DiscardModule(modName.c_str());
  }

  // Clear modules
  m_scriptModules.clear();
}
```

The code that glues the script engine and the Java GUI together is in GPTMain.cpp. It contains the two functions declared in GPTJNILib.java: Initialize and Update as well as a declaration for the global variable gScriptEngine. Due to JNI naming conventions, function signatures are longer than you may be used to. They start with "Java" and then include the package name, followed by the class name, ending with the function name, all separated by underscores.

The Initialize function takes a container of game objects, as sent by the scene player. It resets the script system to start from scratch and proceeds to add each object. Because game objects are sent in the form of an ArrayList of GPTGameObject Java instances, special JNI functions are used to get individual instances and their property values. For example, to get the color of the first object in the gameObjects container, you would write the code shown in Listing 12-20.

Listing 12-20. How to Get a Property Value from a Java Object in C/C++

```
jclass editorGameObjClass =
env->FindClass("com/gametoolgems/gpt/GPTEditorGameObject");

jfieldID gameObjColorField =
env->GetFieldID(editorGameObjClass, "color", "I");

jobject gameObj =
(jobject)env->GetObjectArrayElement(gameObjects, 0);

jint objColor = env->GetIntField(gameObj, gameObjColorField);
```

First, you get a handle on the Java code's GPTEditorGameObject class. The fully qualified name is required, which also includes the package name. Second, you get a handle on the color property of the class by calling the GetFieldID function with the class handle and the name of the property. The last parameter in the GetFieldID function is a way to tell it what the data type is. The "I" means it's an integer type. Next, you use the GetObjectArrayElement function and send it an index of 0 to get the first object in the array list. And last, the color value is obtained by calling the GetIntField function and passing it the object and the handle to the color property. The full code for the Initialize function is shown in Listing 12-21.

Listing 12-21. JNI Initialize Function

```
JNIEXPORT void JNICALL
Java_com_gametoolgems_gpt_GPTJNILib_Initialize(JNIEnv * env,
  jobject obj, jobjectArray objects)
{
  // Reset script engine
  gScriptEngine.Reset();
  //  Initialize script system with scene
  const char* className =
    "com/gametoolgems/gpt/GPTEditorGameObject";

  jclass editorGameObjClass = env->FindClass(className);

  jfieldID goId =
    env->GetFieldID(editorGameObjClass, "id", "I");

  jfieldID goX =
    env->GetFieldID(editorGameObjClass, "x", "F");

  jfieldID goY =
    env->GetFieldID(editorGameObjClass, "y", "F");

  jfieldID goColor =
    env->GetFieldID(editorGameObjClass, "color", "I");

  jfieldID goScript =
    env->GetFieldID(editorGameObjClass,
      "script", "Ljava/lang/String;");

  jsize len = env->GetArrayLength(objects);
  for (int i = 0; i < len; ++i)
  {
    jobject gameObj =
    (jobject)env->GetObjectArrayElement(objects, i);

    jint objId =
      env->GetIntField(gameObj, goId);

    jfloat objX =
      env->GetFloatField(gameObj, goX);

    jfloat objY =
      env->GetFloatField(gameObj, goY);

    jint objColor =
      env->GetIntField(gameObj, goColor);

    jstring objScript =
      (jstring)env->GetObjectField(gameObj, goScript);
```

```
    const char* scriptCode =
      env->GetStringUTFChars(objScript, NULL);
    gScriptEngine.AddGameObject(
      objId, objX, objY, objColor, scriptCode);

    // Release string
    env->ReleaseStringUTFChars(objScript, scriptCode);
  }
}
```

The Update function receives the number of seconds elapsed since the last time you updated, and an empty Java ArrayList, which will be filled with GPTGameObject instances. The script system's Update method is called to run one step on every object, and then the GetUpdatedObjects function is called to collect the updated objects in a std::vector. For every element in the vector, a GPTGameObject instance will be created and added to the ArrayList. And as you saw earlier in the Java GUI code, this is how you draw the updated scene (see Listing 12-22).

Listing 12-22. JNI Update Function

```
JNIEXPORT void JNICALL
Java_com_gametoolgems_gpt_GPTJNILib_Update(
JNIEnv * env, jobject obj, jfloat deltaTime,
jobject objArrayList)
{
  // Update game objects and script system
  gScriptEngine.Update(deltaTime);

  // Get updated game objects
  std::vector<GameObject> gameObjects;
gScriptEngine.GetUpdatedObjects(gameObjects);

// Send updated objects to Java
const char* className =
  "com/gametoolgems/gpt/GPTGameObject";
jclass gameObjectClass =
  env->FindClass(className);

jmethodID gameObjectCtor =
  env->GetMethodID(gameObjectClass,
    "<init>", "(IFFI)V");

jclass arrayListClass =
  env->FindClass("java/util/ArrayList");

jmethodID arrayListCtor =
  env->GetMethodID(arrayListClass, "<init>", "()V");

jmethodID addFunction =
  env->GetMethodID(arrayListClass,
    "add", "(Ljava/lang/Object;)Z");
```

```
for (size_t i = 0; i < gameObjects.size(); ++i)
{
  const GameObject& gameObj = gameObjects[i];
  jobject newGameObj =
    env->NewObject(gameObjectClass,
      gameObjectCtor, gameObj.id,
      gameObj.x, gameObj.y, gameObj.color
      );

  jboolean result =
  env->CallBooleanMethod(objArrayList,
    addFunction, newGameObj);
}
}
```

Test Drive

Hopefully, by working with the code, you now realize the power of this prototyping system. However, the fun part is trying it out, so you will create a very simple scene in a matter of minutes.

Build both the native code and Java code, and run the application on your mobile device or emulator. You should see the scene editor come up. Tap on the colored circle button several times until the green circle appears. Then tap once in the empty scene area, preferably near the top. A green object should appear, and it should have a gray outline, indicating it's selected. Now tap on the Edit Script button. The script editor should come up, with a default script that contains an empty OnUpdate function. You will write code that makes the object move, given a constant velocity. The code should look like that in Listing 12-23.

Listing 12-23. AngelScript Code for the One-Minute Scene

```
float velocity = 100.0f;

void OnUpdate(float dt)
{
  me.y += velocity * dt;
}
```

Now press the Back button on your device twice, once to hide the keyboard and a second time to go back to the scene editor. Tap on the Play Scene button to go to the scene player. When there, press Play and watch the magic happen!

What's Next

While the prototyping tool you just created gives you some power, there are many features it still lacks. Previously I mentioned sending touch input to the scripted objects, creating and destroying objects, and the ability to detect collisions with other objects. Additional features include creating object prefabs before placing them as object instances, using textured sprites instead of colored circles, and a visual scripting system. The important takeaway from this chapter is that the prototyping tool should be bound only by the limits of your own imagination. In other words, the tool's features can grow with every new idea. I invite you to improve it, or reimagine it completely. Hopefully this chapter has sparked an interest in the internal workings of authoring tools, and given you the knowledge to continue learning.

Engineering Domain-Specific Languages for Games

Robert Walter

Programming languages are like musicians. The broader the audience they are addressing, the more popular they can become, even if they are not the best at what they do. While it takes a lot more than a mainstream orientation to stay on top of the charts, it is always a plus to address the wants of the many.

But there is a place for the specialized, too. Just as alternative artists pervade the history of music, domain-specific languages (DSLs) have enjoyed a long tradition in software engineering (a good overview is given in Deursen et al., 2000[1]). While early versions of this kind of programming language like FORTRAN, Lisp, and COBOL evolved over the years to fulfill more generic purposes (thus staying famous), others like SQL, regular expressions, and make became evergreens within their technical domains. Despite their success, however, the concept of engineering and the potential of using DSLs have been relegated to the "academics and theory" shelf for a long time (a good reference on DSL development patterns is given in Mernik et al., 2005[2]). Only recently, a growing interest in software design philosophies like user-centered and domain-driven design, as well as the coming of age of model-driven development methodologies and language workbenches, has led to a new popularity for these elegant tools.

Now, without stressing the music analogy any further, let's take a look at two questions.

1. Why should game developers care about DSLs?

2. How can game developers make use of DSLs?

Naturally, I need to cover some basics first, but I cannot dive too deep into the details of language-oriented programming (LOP) in this chapter. Therefore, those who are new to the field of programming languages and how they work might consider reading the cited literature first.

---

[1] van Deursen, Arie, Paul Klint, and Joost Visser. "Domain-specific languages: an annotated bibliography." SIGPLAN Not. 35 (2000): 26–36.

[2] Mernik, Marjan, Jan Heering, and Anthony M. Sloane. "When and how to develop domain-specific languages." ACM Comut. Surv. Ser. 4. 37 (2005): 316–344.

CHAPTER 13 ■ ENGINEERING DOMAIN-SPECIFIC LANGUAGES FOR GAMES

What Are DSLs?

Object-oriented programming expert Martin Fowler only recently defined the term "domain-specific language" in a very handy way (Fowler, 2010[3]), so let's use his definition in order to discuss the characteristics of DSLs:

> *A DSL is a computer programming language of limited expressiveness focused on a particular domain.*

The purpose of a DSL is to let users write computer instructions in a "natural" way. I knowingly choose the generic term "user" in this context, since DSLs are first and foremost languages designed for domains, not specific user groups. Although domain experts should be involved in the creation of a DSL to make use of their domain knowledge, they do not have to be users of the language. In game development, however, there is a huge potential in empowering designers using DSLs, as you will see later.

Unlike general-purpose languages (GPLs) like C++ and Java, DSLs provide only a limited vocabulary and almost no control structures. Instead, they offer powerful, domain-specific semantics. In short, a DSL features exactly the elements necessary to describe its application field formally (read "completely") and precisely, which makes it easier to learn, even if less expressive, than a GPL. DSLs abstract by making the relevant details of a domain explicit, while omitting the distracting ones. This approach allows developers to address problems right where they occur: in the problem space, instead of manually mapping them to a generic solution space.

Like GPLs, DSLs feature a formal syntax. Thus, a domain-specific program (DSP, a program written in a DSL) can be processed automatically with an interpreter or a generator, for example.

What Does a DSL Look Like?

Bearing the game development process in mind, you can think of a sample language that is tailored to the "interactive dialog" domain. Listing 13-1 shows a language definition using four regular expression rules.

Listing 13-1. Simple Language Definition for Branching Dialog

```
dialog ::= dialogLine dialogLine+ ;
dialogLine := character action ':' STRING ('or' dialogLine)?;
character := ID ;
action := 'asks' | 'says' | 'answers' ;
```

The first rule defines a dialog as a dialogLine followed by at least one or an arbitrary number of additional dialogLine elements (specified through the + symbol). A dialogLine features a character that has to be an identifier (ID), followed by an action that is either the keyword asks, says, or answers. A colon and a STRING (the actual content of the dialog line) follow. The rule for the dialogLine uses optional recursion (the ? symbol indicates optionality) to allow nesting dialog lines. A program written in the language above might look like the one in Listing 13-2. Although the language design in this example is certainly far from perfect, it should give a basic idea of what DSLs can look like.

Listing 13-2. Simple DSP Example for Branching Dialog

```
Robert asks: "So, what do you think of this so far?"
Reader answers: "It looks just great!"
    or
Reader answers: "Not so sure if that might work, but I'll give it a try."
```

---

[3]Fowler, Martin. Domain-Specific Languages. Amsterdam: Addison-Wesley Longman, 2010.

Using proper generators, dialog written in the language of Listing 13-1 can be transformed into different formats. For example, you could create several scripts sorted by characters for the audio recordings, the necessary XML format for the story engine, and a graphical representation such as a dialog tree displaying the dialog's structure. The dialog script becomes the central entity for dialog writing (it is code, after all!). Whenever dialog needs to be changed, the writer changes the DSP and distributes the new version by recompiling the program. This type of centralization represents but one way that DSLs can significantly help to preserve consistency throughout the development process, utilizing the "DRY" principle ("Don't Repeat Yourself," Hunts and Thomas, 1999[4]).

Now, for everyone who might feel the need for a third, more "renegade" reader answer in Listing 13-2, like, "Don't bother me with DSLs. Everyone knows that they are impractical due to the fact that one always needs to build a complete infrastructure for them, like a parser, an editor, and an analyzer, which still would not be comparable to a common IDE," please make do with the second reader answer in Listing 13-2 for now. I'll come back to this issue in a second.

A Categorization of DSLs

There exist different "kinds" of DSLs. A DSL can either be internal or external (Fowler, 2010[5]). This differentiation is useful since internal and external DSLs are not only different in the way they are created and used, they are also usually applied in different contexts, as you will explore in a second. A less rigorous way to categorize DSLs is to consider their technical orientation. Eventually, both ways of categorization should help you to get a better "grip" on the term "DSL."

Internal DSLs

An internal DSL is embedded in a GPL using a limited set of the features of the GPL. Internal DSLs are bound to the grammar of their host language and thus do not need a distinct toolset to be processed. This, of course, constrains the flexibility of syntax design. A good example of an internal DSL is incorporated within the .NET Framework component LINQ. It provides a natural language-like API that utilizes the access to data collections.

A common way of defining an internal DSL is through chained methods. Listing 13-3 illustrates the Method Chaining pattern (compare Fowler, 2010; there are more patterns described to define internal DSLs—take a look at Fowler's book) available in LINQ. The given statement returns a list of selected inventory items in descending order according to their value. Note that this is plain C# code.

Listing 13-3. Example of the Method Chaining Pattern Used in LINQ

```
return inventoryItems
       .Where(item => item.IsSelected)
       .OrderByDescending(item => item.Value);
```

Internal DSLs exploit the advantages of language-like programming interfaces, making code more comprehensible and consequently easier to maintain. In game development, I consider internal DSLs a useful tool to simplify development processes, since many domain experts (visual artists, sound engineers, etc.) do have a technical background and thus, even if they are not intending to use internal DSLs to develop game logic by themselves, are able to understand corresponding programs. This capability introduces interesting possibilities in terms of communication, cooperation, and agile development techniques like pair programming.

---

[4]Hunts, Andrew, and David Thomas. The Pragmatic Programmer. Amsterdam: Addison-Wesley Longman, 1999.
[5]Fowler, Martin. Domain-Specific Languages. Amsterdam: Addison-Wesley Longman, 2010.

External DSLs

Juxtaposed with internal DSLs, external DSLs are self-contained languages featuring their own grammar and a standalone infrastructure. Hence, an external DSL can be tailored exactly to the requirements of the domain, using semantically meaningful keywords and grammar rules. Similar to GPLs, a program written in an external DSL is processed in the form of an abstract syntax tree (AST). As a consequence, one needs to define proper processing tools in order to really benefit from an external DSL. The creation of external DSLs is increasingly supported by tools commonly called language workbenches, like Xtext, MetaEdit+, MPS, and Microsoft's Software Factories, which, among other things, feature rich support for the creation of IDE tooling. For example, based on a single syntax definition file, Xtext creates the corresponding abstract syntax definition file, a fully featured parser, and a serializer, as well as a rich plug-in editor with syntax highlighting, code completion and validation, and quick fixes by default (see Figure 13-1).

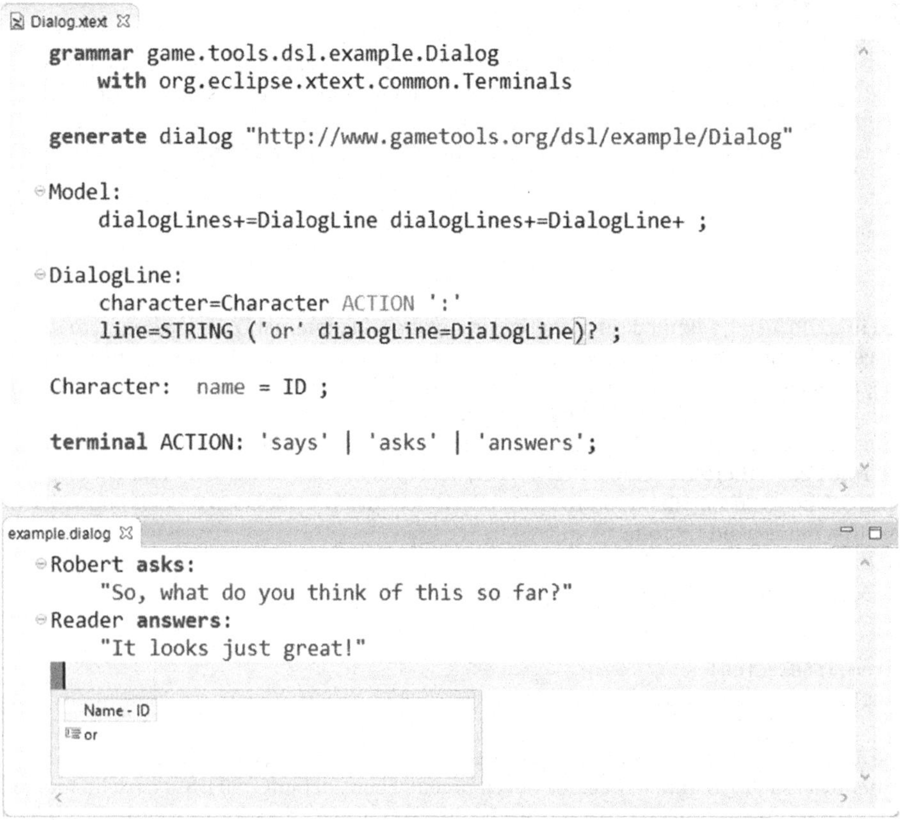

```
Dialog.xtext ⊠
    grammar game.tools.dsl.example.Dialog
        with org.eclipse.xtext.common.Terminals

    generate dialog "http://www.gametools.org/dsl/example/Dialog"

    Model:
        dialogLines+=DialogLine dialogLines+=DialogLine+ ;

    DialogLine:
        character=Character ACTION ':'
        line=STRING ('or' dialogLine=DialogLine)? ;

    Character:  name = ID ;

    terminal ACTION: 'says' | 'asks' | 'answers';
```

```
example.dialog ⊠
    Robert asks:
        "So, what do you think of this so far?"
    Reader answers:
        "It looks just great!"

        Name - ID
        or
```

Figure 13-1. *Dialog language definition in Xtext (top) and complying sample program in generated default editor (bottom)*

Technical Orientation

In addition to their environment, DSLs differ in their technical orientation. This is a qualitative distinction compared to the one above, but it proves useful to understand the potential in the application of DSLs. The internal DSL integrated in LINQ, for example, is a highly technically oriented, internal DSL. It utilizes the ability to query structured data, which can be used for arbitrary application domains. SQL is an example of a technically oriented, external DSL. Altogether, we can categorize DSLs that abstract a technical problem space as highly technically oriented (as has been done similarly by Kleppe, 2008[6]).

In contrast, there are languages that describe non-technical domains. For example, Inform, currently in its seventh installment, features a declarative DSL with a very natural language-like syntax to create interactive fiction applications, as shown in Listing 13-4. Inform 7 abstracts a non-technical domain to allow users to create their own interactive fiction without handling technical issues.

Listing 13-4. Rule Description in Inform 7

```
Instead of throwing something at a closed openable door, say "Or you could just use the handle like
anyone else, of course."
```

Figure 13-2 provides an overview of possible DSL forms of interest in this chapter. While a DSL is either internal or external, the dimension of technical orientation is certainly somewhat blurry, allowing DSLs to address different fields of application. As it is especially hard to think of a popular internal DSL with a low technical orientation, Figure 13-2 shows an example of a made-up language, which could be embedded in C++ to equip characters and set some properties.

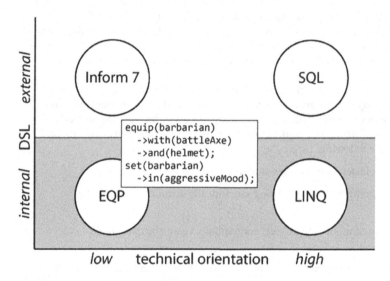

Figure 13-2. *A DSL landscape*

Note that DSLs do not have to be textual, but can be graphical, contain tables, or mix different kinds of representations. Although it is a major decision whether to use a textual or a visual language, this differentiation is of no further concern for the workflow presented here. The decision should always be made individually in a very early phase of language engineering and should depend on which representation best fits the domain at hand.

[6]Kleppe, Anneke. Software Language Engineering: Creating Domain-Specific Languages Using Metamodels. Amsterdam: Addison-Wesley Longman, 2008.

Why Should You Even Care?

As mentioned before, domain-specific languages raise the level of abstraction, which allows you to address problems right where they occur. But what does this mean for game development? Game development combines the artistic challenges of multimedia production with the engineering challenges of IT. Experts from many different disciplines (game design, art, programming, acting, music, and so on) join forces to create and deliver a product. Thereby, the transition from game design to a playable game is arguably the most crucial step to take within a production process.

Game design documents (GDDs) are the common tool used to bridge the gap between design and implementation. However, just as in classic software engineering, document-based development approaches of this kind present several problems. They rely heavily on game designers' ability to communicate their ideas in a comprehensible way, and to understand problems occurring during implementation that call for design changes. These changes must be thoroughly integrated into the GDD. At the same time, development teams must be able to interpret the design document correctly and translate it into code, never missing revisions or ad hoc changes.

It is hard to guarantee consistency throughout a project, especially with larger teams. On a project management level, agile development approaches like Scrum (Schwaber, 1995, Keith, 2010) have been introduced successfully in the last years to address these issues and to compensate for the missing scalability. Utilizing frequent communication ("daily scrums") and short iteration cycles ("sprints"), an empowerment of the development teams as well as a process supervising role ("scrum master") have brought significant benefits to different AAA productions, like Double Fine's Brütal Legend,[7] Valve's Left 4 Dead 2,[8] and Turn 10's Forza Motorsport 3.[9] Still, there is a gaping lack of consistency on the tool level that strengthens the transition from design to implementation, and that is where DSLs fit in.

In the realm of academia, there are different approaches that try to devise generic, formal languages that allow the description of game design per se. Because they need to be able to cover the design of Skyrim as well as Angry Birds, however, their concrete syntax often lacks accessibility and expressiveness, making them inapplicable in practice.

It seems to be a more flexible and hence a more pragmatic approach to allow and utilize both the creation and the application of specific modeling languages that meet the demands of a given game project directly. This way, toolsmiths and developers can facilitate long-established and a "for them approved" terminology as well as an appropriate level of technical orientation and abstraction in the language design. DSLs enable exactly this, and generally, can be an integral tool to support the following:

- The implementation of games in a faster, more precise, and more natural way.

- The communication of game design by creating and using semantically meaningful and at the same time formal models.

- In the case of external DSLs, the integration of high-level content into a game by automated interpretation or (text) generation.

Hence, the main potential of DSLs in game development is to empower non-programmers like game designers and writers. Still, DSLs can be a useful tool for programmers too, not least by fostering interdisciplinary collaboration among the different domain expert groups, but also by writing code on a higher level of abstraction. This approach leads to faster iteration times, a higher consistency throughout the development process, and eventually to higher product quality.

In the following section, you will look at a language engineering workflow that demonstrates how DSLs can be defined and how this process can accompany and enhance game design.

---

[7]Gamasutra. "Postmortem: Behind The Scenes Of Brutal Legend." www.gamasutra.com/view/news/25799/Postmortem_Behind_The_Scenes_Of_Brutal_Legend.php#.UJAn-Gcdx_A.

[8]Nutt, Christian. "Q&A: Valve's Swift On Left 4 Dead 2's Production, AI Boost." Gamasutra. www.gamasutra.com/view/news/25701/QA_Valves_Swift_On_Left_4_Dead_2s_Production_AI_Boost.php#.UJAod2cdx_A.

[9]Graft, Kris. "Racing Evolution: Forza 3 And The Changing Driving Sim." Gamasutra. www.gamasutra.com/view/feature/4144/racing_evolution_forza_3%25%20_and_the_.php.

How to Use DSLs

The categorization of DSLs has shown that their application can be manifold. That is also true in the context of game development. However, instead of a tedious discussion about which application fields might be more or less appropriate for them, you will work through a language engineering workflow. The workflow is intended to let you, as a toolsmith, create languages for your game projects, since you know best which tools fit into your development process. The workflow is therefore knowingly independent from the type of DSL you want to create and the tools you want to use to create your language infrastructure. For illustration purposes, you will consider the creation of a weapon definition language to highlight the steps of the workflow and underline how the language creation process itself can be used in the context of designing aspects of a game. Naturally the example is simplified due to the limited space a book chapter provides.

Language Engineering Workflow

The creation of a domain-specific language is an iterative process, just as the creation of a good game should be. The main assumptions of the language engineering workflow presented here are that there should always be two different kinds of development roles and that the language design should be undertaken from the bottom up.

Figure 13-3 shows the two developer roles in language engineering. First, let's define a domain expert as a person with extensive domain knowledge and expertise. The domain expert is in charge of identifying and defining the entities and semantics of the domain. Domain experts are not in charge of developing the language's actual syntax or any tools for language processing. This responsibility falls to the language engineer, who is a person with extensive knowledge in language design and tool creation for various environments and purposes.

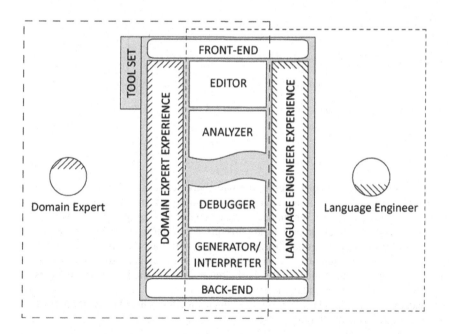

Figure 13-3. Roles and their tasks in language engineering

Depending on the scope of the domain, it is reasonable that more than one domain expert and language engineer participate in the language engineering process. Furthermore, the described tasks of a domain expert can be subdivided into front-end and back-end tasks. This means that there might be a front-end domain expert, for example, a game writer who leads the identification of the requirements for a branching dialog language. One back-end domain expert, a programmer of the story engine, covers the design of the intended outcome and further processing, while another back-end domain expert, a localization manager, determines which information is necessary for voice recording scripts. The language engineers take this information and synthesize it into a language definition and corresponding toolset. The basic workflow with the respective role responsibilities is shown in Figure 13-4.

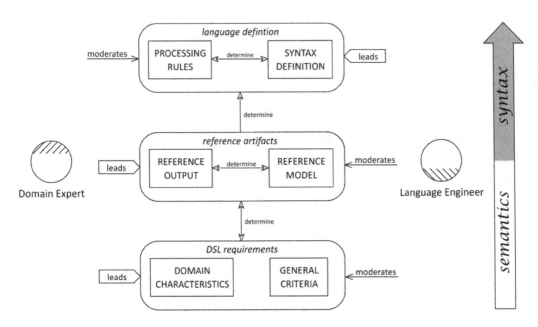

***Figure 13-4.** Bottom-up workflow with role responsibilities*

DSL Requirements

Led by the domain expert(s), the DSL requirements are determined by domain characteristics, which means that proper abstractions of the domain need to be found. The domain characteristics should therefore at least comprise the central domain entities and terms with clearly confined semantics for the given domain. Language engineers should interpret their role in a predictive, hence moderating, way during this phase in order to create both a sound domain outline and a solid foundation for the ultimate language design. As the bidirectional relationship between the DSL requirements and the reference artifacts points out, I propose an iterative process between these two tiers. The DSL requirements are meant to eventually capture the domain so that both domain experts and language engineers are aware of the vocabulary, semantics, purpose, scope, and target group of the domain.

What is called "general criteria" can be derived from language engineering principles as listed in Table 13-1, taken from the book *Software Language Engineering* by Kleppe, 2009.

Table 13-1. *Principles of Language Engineering*

Principle	Description
Simplicity	An easy-to-learn language is easy to use.
Consistency	Choose a suitable design and hold [on] to it.
Flexibility	Give the user flexibility in how to formulate a DSP.
Homogeneity	Show related concepts in the same way and keep them together; show unrelated concepts differently and separately.
Color	Use color sparsely.
Testing	Test the language design on language users.

For this example, you'll look at a fictional language creation process at Fictional Game Studio (FGS), following the toolsmith and language engineer Tobey, working with a game designer called David to create a DSL for defining weapons and their behavior. Tobey is new to the team and does not yet know how the internal processes at FGS work. In a first iteration, David describes the requirements for the language as follows.

David: In our upcoming game, the player will use different kinds of weapons, each with its own abilities and behavior. The goal is to have a simple language that allows us designers to describe the weapons and how to use them. Based on these descriptions, we want to generate different things like a media list for the art department, statistics about the weapons, and the necessary code files so that our game engine can work with the weapons.

Tobey: By "kinds of weapons," do you mean that there will be different weapon classes you want to describe with the language, like Sword and Axe, or do you mean to describe specific weapons like a sword called Slicer, for example?

David: Both! There will be what we call weapon types, like Sword, Dagger, or Axe, which determine distinct abilities for a weapon, like range or how the weapon is handled. Then there will be concrete swords, like a Slicer or an axe called Splitter, which are the actual weapons used by the player.

Tobey: So there is already a fixed set of weapon types?

David: We know that we want to include swords, daggers, and axes, but the language should allow us to define new weapon types during development.

Tobey: This means we need a weapon type description language as well as a weapon description language. How is a weapon type defined?

David: Every weapon type determines if it is a one-handed or a two-handed weapon. What's more, a weapon type is either of short, medium, or long range, and either of slow, medium, or fast velocity.

Tobey: And what abilities do weapons have?

David: Every weapon has a unique name and a unique look. Naturally, a weapon has an attack attribute that determines how much damage the weapon can do. There is also a durability attribute, which determines the weapon's status.

Tobey: What does that mean exactly?

David: Over time, weapons get worse, and durability decreases. When durability becomes zero, the weapon breaks and becomes worthless when used.

Tobey: So weapons get worse over time regardless of whether they are being used?

David: That's actually a good question! The durability was meant to decrease by stroke and a certain probability. However, our game tells a story throughout several decades, so let me discuss this with my team before making a decision.

While the domain expert, David, describes the intention for the language, Tobey needs to ask the right questions to find and define the requirements of the domain at hand. As you can see with the durability property for weapons, the process of defining the language requirements might be used as a tool to reconsider game design itself, although this is not its primary focus, of course. Tobey and David are going to refine this first requirement talk after taking a look at the second layer of the language engineering workflow, namely the reference artifacts.

Reference Model

There are two kinds of ephemeral artifacts that have to be created in the second layer of the language engineering workflow. The intention is to find exemplary instances of the front end (reference models) and the back end (reference output) of the toolset. The reference artifacts should iteratively be developed to enrich and specify the DSL requirements more precisely. In the end, they should include instances for all domain elements in order to cover the domain exemplarily as well as consider language engineering principles (see Table 13-1).

A reference model is a sample program written in the planned language. The central issue is to think of a representation that covers as many of the DSL requirements as possible. Thereby, the reference model serves as a communication platform between domain experts and language engineers in order to combine and manifest their expertise in the language design. In other words, the reference model is the vehicle to map the DSL requirements (layer 1 of the workflow) to the concrete syntax of the language (which will be defined in layer 3). Again, the language engineer should moderate the creation of the reference model, always keeping the tooling of the language in mind. This is where the game designer (as a domain expert) might benefit even more from the language creation process. The task of finding a textual or graphical formal representation that separates a game concept or design from its technical realization in a multi-expert group implicitly leads to a reconsideration of existing design ideas and can validate and render them more precisely and even enhance them. Let's see how Tobey and David are proceeding.

Using pen and paper, David and Tobey start to create reference models for their weapon description language based upon the first DSL requirements.

David: I think I understand what reference models are meant for, but how are we going to approach this?

Tobey: Let's start with the weapon type language. How would you like to define weapon types if we were to be completely free? Go ahead, how would you define the weapon type Halberd, for example?

David: Well, maybe just like this:

```
Halberd is a new weapon type.
```

Tobey: Very good. Now, is it a one-handed or two-handed weapon type? How fast is it? What is its range?

David: This would be a slow, two-handed weapon type of long range.

```
Halberd is a new, slow, long-range, two-handed weapon type.
```

Tobey: I like your language design, since it's extremely readable and explicit. It already contains all the information necessary to define a Halberd. However, it is somewhat verbose, so I would suggest simplifying it a little. Since this is a definition language, I would argue in favor of making this fact explicit in the language, introducing a keyword Define.

```
Define Halberd as a new, slow, long-range, two-handed weapon type.
```

Tobey: Since it's a definition, we can leave out the term "new." What's more, we are going to define weapon types here, so maybe we can also leave out the term "weapon," if you like, to make it handier:

```
Define Halberd as a slow, long-range, two-handed type.
```

After some more corrections and discussion, minding some of the language engineering principles of Table 13-1, they create the following reference model. As you can see, the term *type* is defined to be optional, minding the Flexibility principle.

```
Define type Halberd: slow, long-range, two-handed.
Define Axe: medium, mid-range, one-handed.
Define type Dagger: fast, short-range, one-handed.
```

For defining weapons, they run through a similar process, finally coming up with the reference model shown in Listing 13-5.

Listing 13-5. A Reference Model for Defining Weapons

```
Define Splitter as Axe:
            attack = 16
            durability = 23
          < by stroke: 0.1, 30%
          < by day: 0.2, 50%
Define weapon Needle as Dagger:
            attack = 7
            durability = 20
          < by day: 0.2, 10%
          < by stroke: 0.1, 80%
Define Toothpick as Halberd:
            attack = 38
            durability = 44
          < by day: 0.3, 20%
          < by stroke: 0.2, 30%
```

Weapons are defined by a name and refer to an available weapon type. Similar to the term *type* in the first reference model, *weapon* is declared optional here. After a colon, the weapon properties need to be defined. The attack property is determined by a positive number, while durability is defined by a maximum value as well as two additional value pairs. Each durability decrease is introduced by a lower than symbol. The first pair indicates how much the durability decreases per stroke with a distinct probability, the second pair respectively how much the durability decreases per in-game day, also by a distinct probability. It is up to the designer to decide which decrement behavior is defined first (again, minding the Flexibility principle!).

Reference Output

In general, DSPs can be processed in two different ways. It is possible either to execute a DSP directly with a dedicated interpreter or to process it with a generator, for example, to generate code or configuration files. In the case of generation, the reference output has to represent the desired generated artifacts corresponding to the reference models. The relation between the reference models and the reference output is vital to identifying the processing rules later on. In case of interpretation, the reference output has to mirror the desired results and actions the reference model is intended to evoke. This could be a storyboard displaying how the interpretation of a dialog defined in a DSP should be displayed later on screen. The reference output has to be defined for every target platform and every reference model. That way, the language engineers can derive the processing rules necessary to fill the gap between both abstraction layers. Actually, the gap correlates to the applied degree of abstraction in the DSL. In other words, the processing rules have to add the target platform-relevant details that are omitted by the degree of abstraction of the corresponding DSL. Let's look at the example at FGS again to illustrate this.

For weapon type and weapon description languages at FGS, there are different outputs desired:

- A media list for the art department

- Statistics about the defined weapon types and weapons for the designers

- Configuration files that utilize the weapon types and weapons for the game engine.

You are not going to look at how the different outputs for the DSPs are created from a technical side, but you will examine how the requirements for the processing rules can be identified and refined working with the corresponding domain experts.

Media List

In cooperation with Arthur from the art department, Tobey and David figure out that the media list will be a simplified version of a "weapon program," a simple to-do list, so to speak. Every weapon type needs a 2D icon for the in-game menu, every weapon a 3D model. The idea is that whenever a designer comes up with a new weapon type or weapon, the art department gets an updated to-do list to create a first draft of the necessary asset. In the case of the weapon type language, the art department specifies that they need to know the name of the type (e.g., Dagger) and whether it is a one-handed or two-handed weapon type. In case of the weapon description language, they also need the name-attribute (e.g., Needle) and the corresponding type of that weapon. In order to allow an iterative development process, additions to the weapon program must not override already checked items on the artists' to-do list. The corresponding reference output created by your stakeholders looks like Table 13-2 (the third column is meant to be edited by the artists manually).

Table 13-2. *Reference Output for Art Department*

Weapon Type	One- or Two-handed?	2D Icon Done
Halberd	Two-handed	Yes
Axe	One-handed	No
Dagger	One-handed	No
. . .	. . .	. . .
Weapon	**Type**	**3D Model Done**
Splitter	Axe	Yes
Needle	Dagger	Yes
Toothpick	Halberd	No

Statistics

The statistics for the weapon types and weapons are something that game designers should benefit from. They should help decide which weapons are going to make it into the final game and what kinds of weapons with which properties are missing to finally balance the game's "weapons inventory." Hence, this view should enable the designers to display and compare the already defined weapon types and weapons in terms of their abilities. The information for this view can be directly derived from created weapon programs by parsing the abstract syntax tree. Hence, Tobey and David decide to create an interpreter that displays the statistics for the weapon types using three pie charts. Thereby, the weapon types are counted and compared in terms of their handling (one-handed vs. two-handed), their range (short-, mid-, and long-range) and their velocity (slow, medium, and fast). Moreover, the statistics for weapons should allow designers to ask for the expectable durability of weapons given by their durability properties. Figure 13-5 shows a draft for the statistics view.

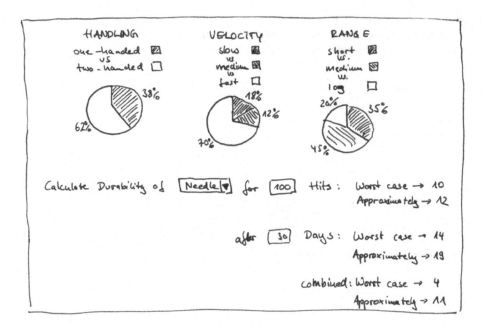

Figure 13-5. *Reference output for statistics view*

While the upper half of the statistics view is not editable, designers are meant to insert a weapon's name, the number of hits, and the number of days in order to see the weapon's worst case and expected behavior. Naturally, you could include a lot more statistical features based on the data of a weapons program.

Configuration File(s)

For the implementation to generate, David and Tobey talk to Paul, the senior programmer of the team. Paul shows Tobey how FGS' in-house game engine manages in-game items in general and how they intend to integrate the modeled weapons into this system. The abstract concept of weapon types is realized in the engine by an abstract class called WeaponType. The code generator is now in place to generate a subclass for every designed weapon type that sets its properties and prepares the necessary method stubs (see Figure 13-6). Moreover, every designed weapon is mapped to an object instance of the corresponding weapon type. Therefore, the generator needs to create a simple XML file that serves as configuration file for the game engine, as shown in Listing 13-6.

Listing 13-6. Excerpt of Reference Output XML Configuration File

```
<Weapons>
    <Weapon id="Splitter">
        <Type>Axe</Type>
        <Attack>16</Attack>
        <MaxDurability>23</MaxDurability>
        <DurabilityBehavior>
            <Day value="0.1" probability ="30" />
            <Stroke value="0.2" probability ="50" />
        </DurabilityBehavior>
    </Weapon>
    ...
</Weapons>
```

Note that the class diagram in Figure 13-6 is not the created reference output but gives an overview of the classes that need to be generated for the corresponding reference model. The reference model would be an actual implementation of at least one of the classes in the target language, such as C++.

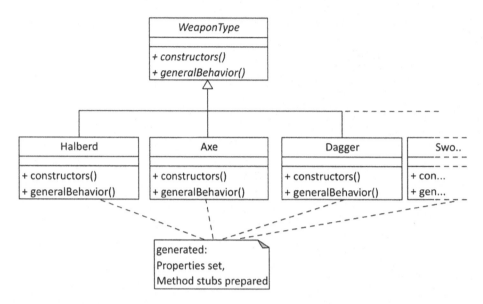

Figure 13-6. *Class diagram illustrating the classes that need to be generated*

Language Definition

The language definition and the processing rules are directly derived from the reference artifacts. The language engineers have to identify syntax rules and static semantics based on the reference models for the language. The creation of the generators and/or interpreters should not be performed at the very end, but iteratively with the language definition, since some requirements of the processing might influence the language implementation. Furthermore, depending on the technology used to create the language toolset, small adaptations—in comparison to the reference model—are inevitable in language design. However, the language engineers should always confer with the domain experts in order to find an adequate solution in case of changes. In order to make external DSLs really applicable, IDE support is necessary. Language workbenches support the creation of smart editors, which, for example, feature syntax highlighting, text completion, and syntax analysis by default.

Just like in GPLs, the abstract syntax is the structural description of a DSL. In its representation as an abstract syntax tree (AST), a DSP can be processed by a parser. The user, however, writes DSPs using a concrete syntax, featuring keywords in a distinct notation. A concrete syntax thereby always conforms to an abstract syntax. Hence, it is possible to create several concrete syntax definitions for the same abstract syntax, for example, a visual and a textual representation for different use cases.

Given the reference artifacts from the last section, Tobey and David are now able to derive the grammar for their languages as well as create the processing rules and tools for the interpreters and generators they need. To illustrate how the grammar can be derived from the reference models, you use the Xtext grammar language to create the weapon type definition language. Considering the reference model again, you can derive that weapon types are defined by a sequence of single weapon type definitions:

```
Define type Halberd: slow, long-range, two-handed.
Define Axe: medium, mid-range, one-handed.
Define type Dagger: fast, short-range, one-handed.
```

The reference model in this example holds three of these weapon type definitions, but in practice there might be an arbitrary number of definitions per file. You can derive a rule that your Model consists of an arbitrary number of TypeDefinitions:

```
Model: typeDefinitions+=TypeDefinition* ;
```

In Xtext, this line means that you have a root element called Model that holds a list of elements of type TypeDefinition. Now, how is TypeDefinition defined? Every single definition starts with the keyword Define, optionally followed by the keyword type. After that, an identifier has to follow. After a colon, the three properties for a weapon type have to be declared. In Xtext, this can look like Figure 13-7.

Figure 13-7. *Language definition (concrete syntax) for weapon types in Xtext (top), showing the automatically generated abstract syntax as ecore model (bottom)*

Similarly, you can derive the grammar rules for the weapon definition language. For the different outputs suggested in the example above, the description of the corresponding implementation would go beyond the scope of this chapter and might well cost a lot of resources.

Conclusion

Domain-specific languages are a powerful tool to abstract the core of a problem from technical or unrelated constraints. For game development, they offer different possibilities to be usefully applied. They can bridge the gap between game design and its implementation by empowering game designers and writers to formally describe parts of a game, meaning to program it. The creation process alone can help to validate, refine, and enhance existing game designs, making the process itself a tool to find precise game design descriptions. Using generators or interpreters, the formal structure of DSLs enables all kinds of possibilities for processing domain-specific programs. Generators might be used to transform a DSP automatically into another, usually more specific format, like C++ code or XML files to free programmers from tedious and error-prone tasks. DSPs might as well be interpreted directly to simulate and evaluate modeled behavior, like playing through an interactive dialog, or to derive additional information from a DSP in real-time, like the in-game item statistics shown in this example. Last, but not least, internal DSLs can be used to make programming interfaces more comprehensible to non-programmers, opening up new possibilities for pair programming, something that, unfortunately, could not be handled in more detail in this chapter.

The language creation process itself can be used to communicate and reconsider a game's design iteratively, as has been shown by the example in this chapter. Game designers can incorporate design rules into the DSL, making the design independent from concrete implementations—an especially important consideration for multiplatform games and/or game series. Once defined, game designs (using a formal language) can be distributed to different platforms with proper generators. Design changes need only be implemented once and can be distributed automatically to all platforms. At the same time, programmers can integrate their domain knowledge into (code) generators so that boilerplate programming tasks are performed automatically with a constant level of quality.

Yet DSLs are no silver bullet for game development. It must still be proven whether the proposed application fields work in practice. A major downside of external DSLs is that one needs to create a corresponding toolset in order to make use of a language. Hence, it is always necessary to consider whether the investment of creating such a tool actually pays off in the intermediate and long term. However, given the state of the art of modern language workbenches that support the implementation of DSLs nowadays, and the fact that there is quite regularly the need to create specific tools in the context of new game projects, it seems only reasonable to consider creating and using DSLs more frequently in the future.

Index

Get the eBook for only $10!

> Now you can take the weightless companion with you anywhere, anytime. Your purchase of this book entitles you to 3 electronic versions for only $10.

This Apress title will prove so indispensible that you'll want to carry it with you everywhere, which is why we are offering the eBook in 3 formats for only $10 if you have already purchased the print book.

Convenient and fully searchable, the PDF version enables you to easily find and copy code—or perform examples by quickly toggling between instructions and applications. The MOBI format is ideal for your Kindle, while the ePUB can be utilized on a variety of mobile devices.

Go to www.apress.com/promo/tendollars to purchase your companion eBook.

Apress®
THE EXPERT'S VOICE™